作者近期拳照
Author's Latest Photo

作者近期拳照
Author's Latest Photo

陈正雷老师正在习练静养功

Practising the Chen Style Taichi Qi Gong

2001年同儿子陈斌在太行山练习推手

Pushing hands with his son, chen Bin, in Tai Hang Mountain, 2001

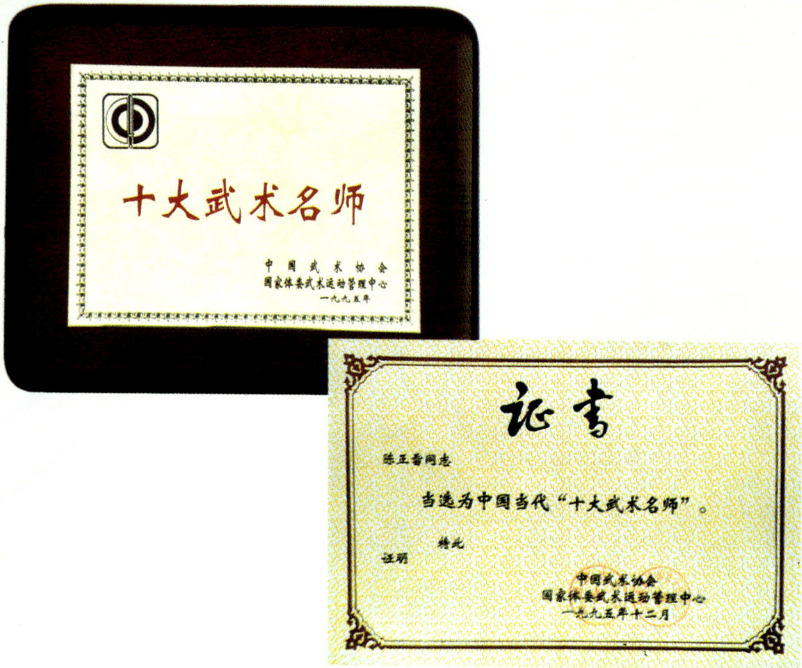

1995 年被中国武术协会评为《中国当代十大武术名师》称号

Be awarded the title of "Ten Famous Top Masters of Wushu of present China" by Chinese Wushu Association in 1995.

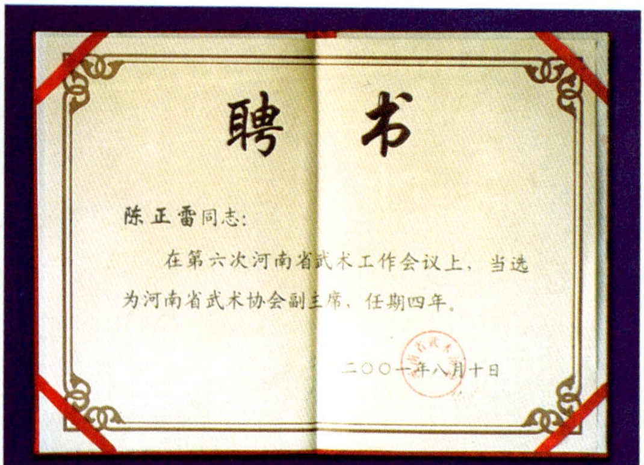

2001 年被选为河南省武术协会副主席

Be elected Vice Chair-man of Henan Wushu Association

1994 年（在台湾讲学）被台湾武术界誉称“登峰造极”

Be awarded the title of "The Peak of Taiji" by Taiwan Wushu circle in 1994

1998 年在英国讲学照

Teaching in the UK in 1998

2000 年在美国讲学照
Teaching in the US in 2000

1999 年在意大利讲学照
Teaching in Italy in 1999

1993 年在马来西亚讲学照
Teaching in Malaysia in 1993

2001 年陈正雷老师参加香港太极拳万人大汇演
Performance on the ceremoney of HK Mass Taiji Practice in 2001

2001 年第三届国际陈氏太极拳培训班照

With his students of 3rd international Chen Taiji Training Class, 2001

The Chen – Style Taijiquan For Life Enhancement

Written by Chen Zhenglei
Translated by Xu Hailiang

Zhongzhou Classic Publishing House

陈氏太极拳
养　生　功

陈　正　雷　著
徐　海　亮　翻译

中州古籍出版社

Developing the Traditional Life Enhancement from China (Preface)

By Mr. Xu Cai, ex-chairman of Asian Wushu Federation

Writing the preface of the *Chen-Style Taijiquan for Life Enhancement* written by Chen Zhenglei, I recalled the coincidence ten years ago in Chenjiagou. It was still cold March that I ran into an American youth. During the conversation, I knew that he was an English teacher in Huanghe University and he loved Taijiquan deeply that he had lived there for almost two months. Then I asked him if he could adapt to the living condition, the fair-hair youth answered that in order to learn Taijiquan better he was able to surmount the poor condition. His words touched me deeply—to pursue Chinese Wushu culture a foreigner beared such poor living condition and learned Taijiquan earnestly. How commendable it is! It was a pity that our conversation was quite short, and I shook him good-bye in the abstruse contemplation. During the last ten years, Chenjiagou, the original place of the Chen-Style Taijiquan, has welcomed numerous foreign friends to practice Taijiquan. Furthermore, Wenxian International Taijiquan Annual Meeting has been held for several times, and nowadays Chen-Style Taijiquan is getting more and popular in the world. I believe, as the host of Taijiquan, Chenjiagou, Wenxian County, China should stick to contributing the fruits of Wushu culture to the world. Chen Zhenglei making the inherited Taiji Qigong public is a new fruit of exploiting and collecting Taijiquan culture, which is worthy congratulating.

All the time, I regard Taijiquan as a gem for stronger body as well as a new star for health building. There is a saying from foreign scholar that the future century is health-building century, which is quite reasonable. Viewing from the tendency of the social development, the longevity of humans is getting longer and longer. Our country owning 1,200 million populations will enter the period of aged society. There is an old Chinese saying that it is rare that when people get 70 years old, however, presently more and more people are older than 70. Japan is the life-longest country in the world, where female are averagely 80 and male are 75. Besides, people are averagely over 70 in many places in China. Indeed, the longevity of humans is growing with the development of society. At present, many scientists are studying the limitation of humans' longevity from different aspects. Some scientists hold that the longevity of humans should be 125 to 175 from the view of the growth period of animals, yet some believe that humans should be older than 120 years with calculating the times of cell division. Although this is just some scientific calculation, the real life is telling us that human longevity is getting longer and longer. Because of this tendency , health building and life enhancement has turned into a significant worldwide topic. In the health-building century, to practice Taijiquan is an excellent way for personal health building.

14 years ago, John Naisbitt, the famous American futurologist wrote a book named *Megatrends*. In his book, when describing the new health-building prospect he mentioned that people would turn from being assisted by medical instruments into self-help, and carry out self-dependent self health building. At that time, he didn't refer to Taijiquan the gem for self health care. However, in his new book *Megatrends* of Asia completed last October, when mentioning "the eastern and western harmony", he told us "the West was inputting the thought mode and conventional concept", "yoga and Chinese medicine occupy the most energy of about 50-year-old house women", and "80-year-old eastern people and 30-year-old western people practice Taijiquan together" in the park. He also said "the real East fans have entered the second level of the Eastern intelligence". In the items of the book he also asked to "Sitting-quietly method of Taoism, not to mention Qigong the 4-thousand-year enhancement method for inside energy". Nowadays, as the Eastern intelligence, the traditional techniques of health building and life enhancement— Taijiquan, Qigong, Sitting-quietly method, etc. is much more acknowledged and enjoyed by the West.

The resource of traditional Chinese life enhancement is traced at least back to the late primeval society. In the early Qin Dynasty, Laozi and Zhuangzi claimed tranquil could cultivate spirits, and Hanfeizi claimed that movement could build form and Tuna, Daoyin could benefit health and regimen. At that period, the concept of being in harmony with nature, actively adjusting for health and longevity primarily formed the system of conventional Chinese health building. In the idea of traditional regimen, energy, Qi, spirit are regarded as the three treasures of body. People who study Wushu for life enhancement take "cultivating energy, Qi and spirit inside, excising hands, eyes, and body outside" as the motto and also emphasize cultivating as well as strengthening inside and outside, which is exactly traditional Chinese complete view of keeping-fit and health care. Taijiquan is not only the regimen technique for removing disease and health building, but also the combat skill for strengthening body and self-protection. In the age of health-building century, people pay much more attention to the function for removing disease and health building of Taijiquan. Chen Zhenglei systematizes Chen-Style Taijiquan for health building and life enhancement, absorbing the essence of Chen-Style Tajiquan in the aspects of health building and medicine, integrating will, Qi, form and respiration, making people and nature sense each other so as to reach consistency. Without doubt, this set of techniques of health building and life enhancement will bring benefit to people inside and outside China. I earnestly wish besides practicing and teaching exercise, masters of Chinese Wushu and Qigong, regimen scholars make dee-

per researches into traditional Chinese health building and greater contribution to humans' health care!

March 1996 Beijing

弘扬祖国传统养生术（序）

徐　才

在提笔为陈正雷先生所著《陈氏太极拳养生功》作序时，我想起了十年前在陈家沟的一次偶遇。那时还是寒意未消的阳春三月，我在陈家沟练功房前边的一间小屋里碰上一位美国青年，搭起话来，知道他是在黄河大学教授英语的老师，因酷爱太极拳在这里已经住了快两个月了。我当即问他，这里居住和饮食条件你都能适应吗？这位金发碧眼的年轻人说，为了学好太极拳，能够克服艰苦的生活条件。听后我很感动。我想，一个外国人为了追求中国的武术文化，竟能忍受艰苦生活，孜孜不倦地习练太极拳功夫，真是难能可贵。可惜我们的对话时间甚短，我带着一缕深沉的思索同他握别了。十年来，陈氏太极拳发源地的陈家沟，每年都迎来众多的外国朋友习练太极拳，温县国际太极拳年会也已办了数届，陈氏太极拳正在世界风靡。我以为，作为太极拳发源地的陈家沟、温县、中国，需要不断地拿出武术文化的结晶献给世界。陈正雷先生把祖传的太极内功（气功）养生法公诸于世，这是挖掘整理太极拳文化的一个新成果，值得祝贺。

我一直认为太极拳是今日人类增进健康的一块瑰宝，又是明日人类保健的一颗新星。国外有的学者说，未来的世纪是保健的世纪，这是颇有道理的。从社会发展的趋势看，人的寿命越来越长。我们这个拥有12亿人口的国家，到下世纪初也将进入老龄化社会。古话说，人生七十古来稀，现在则是人生七十今来多了。日本是世界上最长寿的国家，女性平均寿命已达80岁，男性已达75岁。我国许多地方人均寿命也已超过70岁。的确，人类的寿命随着社会的进步在不断增长。世界上许多科学家，从不同的角度研究人类的寿限。有的科学家从动物生长期角度研究人的寿命，认为人的寿限应是125—175岁。有的科学家从细胞分裂次数推算人的寿命，认为人的寿限应在120岁以上。尽管这只是一些科学推算，但现实生活昭告我们，人类的寿龄确是在不断增长。随着这种趋势的发展，人类的保健养生就成为一个世界性的重要课题。老年人需要保健，中年人、青年人以及少年、儿童都需要保健。在保健的世纪，太极拳是个人们自我保健的良好手段。

美国著名的未来学家约翰·奈斯比特14年前在一度轰动全球的《大趋势》一书中，描绘"新的保健图景"时提出，人们将从依赖医疗机构帮助转变到自助，"实行自力更生的自我保健"。当时他没有提到太极拳这个自我保健的瑰宝。但在去年10月完成的他的新著《亚洲大趋势》中说到"东西方的和谐"时指出，"西方人正在从东方'进口'思维方式和传统观念"，"瑜伽和中医占去了50岁左右家庭妇女的多半精力"，"公园里80岁的东方人和30岁的西方人一起打着太极拳"。他还进一步说到西方人从东方"进口"的范围远不止这些，"真正的东方迷们已经进入东方智慧的第二层次"。他在条例中提到"研究道家的打坐，更别提那已有四千年历史的内功修炼方法——气功了"。

是啊，太极拳、气功、打坐等中国传统的自我保健养生术，作为东方智慧越来越被西方人认识和享用了。

中国传统养生术的起源，至迟可以追溯到原始社会末期。到了先秦时期，老子、庄子主张清静养神，韩非子等主张动以养形，以吐纳、导引保健养生。那个时期提出的顺应自然，主动调摄，以求康寿的观点初步形成了中国传统养生学的体系。在传统养生思想中，把精、气、神视为人身的三宝。习武养生者把"内练精气神，外练手眼身"当作座右铭，强调内外兼修，壮内强外。这正是中国传统的整体健身观和养生观。太极拳既是祛病保健的养生功夫，又是强身防身的技击功夫。如今在保健的世纪向我们走来的时刻，人们越来越重视太极拳的祛病保健养生的作用了。陈正雷先生整理的陈氏太极拳养生功，摄取了陈氏太极拳在健身养生及医疗保健方面的精华，把意、气、形和呼吸有机地结合在一起，使人与自然相互感应，达到天人合一。相信这套功法是会给中外人士保健养生带来福音的。我衷心祝愿我国的武术家、气功家、养生家在练功、授功之余，深入挖掘整理祖国的传统养生术，为人类的保健做出更大的贡献！

一九九六年三月于北京

Foreword

With the development of reform and opening and the progress of social economy, people's living standard is continuously improving, and daily work and lives gradually electricitize, computerize, automatize, which greatly lessens people's physical exercises. Whereas, as physical exercises are getting fewer, the body function of men is getting worse and worse. Therefore, recently the tide of learning Wushu and Qigong is approaching.

In last centuries, Taijiquan, occupying an extremely important status in people's minds, has been widely favored because of the function of health building and self-protection, it even has spread overseas. It is well known that Taijiquan is able to practice bones and muscles, smooth Jingluo (main and collateral channels in the body), adjust nerves and remove diseases. I practice Taijiquan since I was a child, so I know the essence of Taijiquan is its special Qigong, which obviously help to health building. Hence, although this internal exercise is seldom spread outside, in order to improve the health quality of people, it can promote all citizens to take part in exercises, serve society and people, I especially publish the regimen of family inherited Taiji Qigong, and hope to contribute to the health of humans.

Taiji, born from Wuji (polelessness), it was divided into Liangyi, changed into Sancai, appeared Sixiang, finally evolved the Eight Diagrams to the infinity. Qigong is the new term appeared in recent years, which is synonymy with internal exercise in the Wushu theory. In the prevalence of Taiji Wushu, the internal exercise (Qigong) of Taijiquan has been emphasized by Taiji masters and is the stress of Taijiquan. Ancestors always claimed Taijiquan was internal school boxing, which required the practicers Wushu to collect air so as to cultivate energy, to hold the energy to Dantian, to make use of inside vigor change to spirit, to return to void, to return to original purity and simplicity, and to return to emptiness. Heaven, earth and human integrating into one, the merger of Yin and Yang and heaven, earth and human is joined with nature is the ultimate goal of training internal exercise (Qigong).

There is an old saying "cultivating the root, leaves get exuberant by itself, moistening the resource, a stream become longer by itself". The internal exercise of Taiji is based on the same reason. I wish to share and study it with Taiji fans together.

This book introduces *The Chen-Style Taijiquan for Life Enhancement*, *The Taiji Skills of Preserving Vital Energy* (*The Sitting Method*, *The Stake Exercise Method*) and *The Cream Eighteen Forms of Chen-Style Taijiquan*. In addition, in this book, the methods are clear and the words are concise, making it easy to learn. Taijiquan especially takes better effect to the people who suffer from chronic diseases like neurasthenia, high blood pressure, heart disease, indigestion, arthritis, etc. without much ginger.

Chen Zhenglei

February 1996

前言

随着改革开放的逐步深入，社会经济的长足发展，人民的生活水平正在不断提高，日常工作和生活正在逐步向电器化、电脑化、自动化发展，它大大减轻了人们的体力劳动，然而文明病也随之而来，由于身体活动少，人们的体质机能逐渐下降。因此，近些年来掀起了学武健身及气功热的高潮。

数百年来，一直在人们心目中占有极重要地位的“太极拳”，以其健身养生与技击防身的良好作用，深受人们喜爱，且已流传于海内外。其活络筋骨、疏通经络、调解神经、祛病延年之功效，已得世人所公认。笔者自幼习练太极拳，深知太极拳精髓之内家气功，对健康人体之功效显著。为此，虽本功法鲜少外传，但为提高人们健康素质，促进全民健身运动，服务于社会大众，特将祖传的太极内功(气功)养生法公诸于世，希望能为人类的健康事业做出贡献。

太极始于无极，再分两仪而化三才，由三才显四象，演变八卦于无穷，气功者乃近几年之新名词，原在武学中与内功同义，在太极武术流传中，太极内功(气功)一直为历代太极先师所重视，亦为太极拳术中重心所在，故人常称太极拳为内功拳，旨在要求练拳者懂得采气培元，守丹起功，由体内精气化神还虚，以求能返朴归真，由太极而归于无极。所谓天地人合一，阴阳合融，天地人与大自然混为一体，即是为太极内功（气功）修炼之终极目标。

古人云："培其根则枝叶自茂，润其源则流脉自长。"太极内功则为"培根润源"之良方，愿能与热爱太极之人士共同参研分享。

本书所介绍的陈氏太极拳养生功、太极培元养气法（静坐养气法、桩功聚气法）以及陈氏太极拳精要十八式，方法清晰，言简意赅，简便易学，尤对神经衰弱、高血压、心脏病、消化不良、关节炎等慢性病效果甚佳，能起到事半功倍之良效。

作者　陈正雷

一九九六年二月

Introduction to the Chen-style Taijiquan

In the late Ming Dynasty, Taijiquan was created by a garrison commander Chen Wangting the ninth generation of the Chen Family in Chenjiagou, Wenxian County in Henan Province. Based on the inherited family Wushu and the theory of Yin and Yang in *Yijing*, combining Chinese medicine Jingluo Theory, Daoyin and Tuna, Chen Wangting comprehensively initiated a set of Taijiquan, which not only has the quality of Yin and Yang, but also is characterized that with activity and looseness, some movements were energetic while others were gentle, and some rapid while others slow. As being in correspondence with human physiology and the nature operation rules, it was named as "Taijiquan". It is unknown that Taijiquan originally was passed down only in the Chen Family. Until the fourteenth generation when Chen Changxing handed down to Yang Luchan, it began to spread widely in the society. In the long run, Taijiquan developed into four representative, different main styles, including Yang style, Wu style, Wu style, and Sun style.

In the last centuries, Chen-style Taijiquan has still kept the characteristics of ancient Taijiquan, which is characterized that hardness and softness moving in harmony, equaling stress the

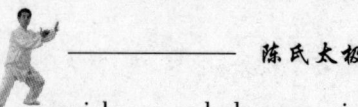

quickness and slowness, jumping and leaping, relaxing and nimble, springing and shaking, and with the practice method of twining force. It is celebrated in the Wushu field for its distinctive value of health building and actual combat technique, also favored enthusiastically by people. At present, Chen-style Taijiquan has spanned China and gone forward to the world, becoming the important bridge between Chinese and foreign friends. The ancient Chen-Style Taijiquan takes a new look and uniquely promoted the outstanding fruits of conventional Chinese culture to people all around the world. Besides it also takes active effects in flourishing economy. Certainly, the Chen-style Taijiquan will make greater dedications to the health of whole human being, and finally becoming the shared treasure of whole human being.

陈氏太极拳简介

太极拳是明末战将，河南温县陈家沟陈氏第九代陈王庭，在家传拳术的基础上，依据“易经”阴阳之理，中医经络学说及导引、吐纳术，综合性地创造了一套具有阴阳性质、刚柔相济、快慢相间，松活弹抖的特色，以及符合人体生理规律和大自然的运转规律的拳术运动，故名“太极拳”。起初，太极拳只在陈氏家族内部流传，鲜为人知。到陈氏十四代陈长兴时，传给河北永年人杨露禅，以后在社会上慢慢流传开来。太极拳在长期流传发展中，逐步演化成具有代表性、风格特点又各不相同的杨、吴、武、孙四大流派。

数百年来，陈氏太极拳仍保留着古太极拳那种刚柔相济、快慢相间、窜蹦跳跃、松活弹抖的特色以及缠绕螺旋的运气方法，并以其卓越的健身养生与技击价值著称于武坛，深受人们喜爱。现在，陈氏太极拳已跨出国门，风靡世界，成为中国人民与世界人民友好交往的重要桥梁。古老的陈氏太极拳正以其崭新的风貌、独有的方式向世界各族人民传播中华民族传统文化的优秀成果，并在繁荣经济方面发挥着积极作用。陈氏太极拳必将为全人类的健康事业做出更大贡献，成为全人类的共同瑰宝。

Contents

目录

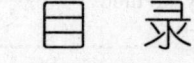

Chapter One The Principles of the Chen-Style Taijiquan for Life Enhancement

第一章 陈氏太极拳养生功功理

The Chen-Style Taijiquan for Life Enhancement originates from the Chen-Style Taijiquan, which is the essence of the Chen-Style Taijiquan in the aspects of medical treatment and health protection. It adopts the special method of taking energy, collecting energy, condensing energy, condensing will of the traditional Chen-Style Taijiquan, and it combines will, energy, action and breath together. At the same time it gets rid of the hardest actions in the former Chen-Style Taijiquan, therefore it has the advantages of getting energy quickly, feeling energy strongly, removing diseases and building body effectively, etc. This exercise has no mistakes, no side effects, and is beneficial to cure the chronic diseases such as high blood pressure, heart trouble, arthritis, neurasthenia, gastric ulcer, and so on. Exercising Taijiquan isn't restricted by place and time, whether old or young.

陈氏太极拳养生功(以下简称养生功),源于陈氏太极拳,是陈氏太极拳在健身养生及医疗保健方面的精华。它择取陈氏

太极拳独特的采气、集气、炼气、炼意方法，把意、气、形和呼吸有机地结合在一起，同时又舍去了陈氏太极拳套路中的高难动作，因而具有得气快、气感强、祛病强身效果好而又方便易学等优点。本功法无偏差、无副作用，对高血压、冠心病、骨质增生、神经衰弱、胃肠官能症等慢性病都有较好疗效，且不受场地、时间等条件限制，男女老少皆宜。

Section I The Features of the Exercise
第一节 功法特点

The Chen-Style Taijiquan for Life Enhancement combines movement with stillness, internal exercises with outside exercises, action with spirit. When exercising, under the precondition of easy, calm and natural state, and the principle of "once move, all move", we can make sense, will, action and breath cooperate together and therefore reach the level of interfusion of human and nature, collect energy from heaven and earth to nourish our body, eliminate the sources of diseases, improve health and wisdom, and further prolong life. Through exercising insistently, the energy can be assembled at Dantian more and more abundantly, and further form the largest and strongest positive energy naturally to culture morality and edify sentiments. Such vast energy can make the effect of health building and medical treatment. When used for self-defense and preventing from enemies, it can produce strong striking force, which is enough to shock the opponent's internal organs wounded. This exercise, which is not restricted by the forms of fist and foot, reacts sensitively and can change action according to situations.

养生功动静结合,内外兼修,形神合一。练功时,在松静自然的前提下,贯穿一动无有不动的原则,使意识、动作、呼吸三者密切配合,人与大自然融为一体,采集天地间清灵之气营养身体,同时排出体内病、浊之气,以增进健康,益智延年。通过持久练功,元气会渐渐聚集于丹田,进而充实,饱满,壮大,自然养就至大至刚的浩然正气,以涵养道德,陶冶情操,坦荡胸怀。这种浩然正气施于自身,可收强身及医疗保健功效;用之防身御敌,则产生强大的冲击力量,足以震伤对方的五脏六腑。本功法反应敏捷,随机应变,具有出于自然而不拘泥于拳脚的形式招数。

Section II The Functions of Health Improvement and Strengthening Body

第二节 健身养生作用

1. Preserving health of the nerve system, improving the ability of reacting to external stimulation

People's normal actions are controlled by nerve system. The cooperation between various muscle teams, muscle actions and organ actions, the cooperation between various systems and the cooperation between inside and outside circumstances, are all controlled by brain cortex. When practicing this exercise, you should keep stillness and spiritual tranquility. If so, you will be able to strengthen the ability of controlling your own will, decrease disturbance from the outside, and make excitement and suppression courses in your brains happen alternately and rhythmically. So excitement and suppression cooperate accurately, and your sensors can receive outside messages exactly. Because of the improvement of the functions of sense and consciousness, human body will improve its ability of active reactions, and become more sensitive to the message of languages and words. This is good for forming conditioned reflex and perfecting the second message system, so you will be able to learn cultural knowledge or grasp the key of actions and techniques more accurately and quickly. The people who often exercise this, will own plenty of energy, clear brains, systematical thought, and his working enthusiasm and efficiency will be improved distinctly.

The exercising method of combining consciousness with action will strengthen diffusibility of nerve system and make the actions between nerve centrums more cooperative. That is, for an instance, movement centrum in brain cortex and the second message system are all in the state of high excitement, but the other parts of the cortex are in the state of protective suppression, which will make the brain rest sufficiently, and dispel fatigue quickly. For persons with chronic diseases, sufficient rest of the brain cortex will get rid of the pathologic focus of chronic diseases, remove the feedback reactions of the disease focus, improve the health level, and reach the aims of a radical cure.

As we all know, emotion is related to health closely. The mood of optimism is good for health, but when seven moods of happiness, anger, worry, thoughtfulness, sorrow, fear, surprise are too excessive, they will bring harm to us. "The seven moods" are internal causes that make people ill, for example, too much happiness harms heart, anger harms liver, worry and thoughtfulness harm spleen, sorrow harms lungs, fear harms kidneys, surprise harms gallbladders, etc. When the seven moods are excessive, our body will be attacked by pathogenic sources of wind, coldness, hotness, dampness, dryness, and inflammation. We will be attacked from both inside and outside together, and at last be ill. Therefore《The Sutra of Internal Medicine》emphasizes spiritual tranquility, which is the request of the exercise. Tense, busy and quick modern city life brings about many negative effects such as tense mind, whiny mood, miscellaneous thought, and so on, which even to some degree effect health and decrease the working efficiency. In order to alleviate tension of mind and pressure, make the emotional actions placid and steady, decrease the internal elements causing diseases, and improve heath level at last, the exercise requires quietness and inaction, controlling yourself by will and making body and spirit relax as possible as you can.

一、保健神经系统，提高应激反应能力

正常人的一切活动，都是在神经系统的控制下进行的。身体各肌群之间，肌肉活动与内脏活动之间，各器官、系统及器官与系统之间的密切配合以及身体内外环境的协调统一，都有赖于大脑皮质的调节作用。练功时要求清静用意，精神内守，可以增强意念控制能力，减少外界干扰，使本体感觉皮质部位的兴奋抑制过程在一定时间内能严格地、有节奏地转移，兴奋与抑制更加精确地配合，感受器能更准确地摄取外界信息。由于感官知觉功能的提高，增强了人体的积极性反应，对语言、文字等信息也更加敏锐，利于形成条件反射，第二信号系统更趋完善。这样，无论学习文化知识，还是掌握动作技术，都会迅速准确。经常练养生功的人，会感到精力充沛，头脑清晰，思维极有条理，工作热情和工作效率明显提高。

意识和动作相结合的练功方法，会增强神经系统的扩散性，使协同中枢之间的活动更加协同一致，即大脑皮质的运动中枢及第二信号系统处于高度兴奋状态，而皮质的其他部位处于保护性抑制状态，使大脑得到充分的休息，人体很快就消除了疲劳。对慢性病患者来说，由于大脑的充分休息，打破了慢性病的病理兴奋灶，消除了病灶的反馈影响，提高了健康水平，最终达到根治慢性病的目的。

我们知道，人的情感活动与健康关系密切。乐观向上的心境有益于健康，而过度的喜、怒、忧、思、悲、恐、惊等七情活动都会给健康带来危害。“七情”是使人致病的内因。如过喜伤心、

怒伤肝、忧思伤脾、悲伤肺、恐伤肾、惊伤胆等。在七情过度时，外界的风、寒、暑、湿、燥、火等六淫就会乘虚而入，内外交感，造成疾病。所以《内经》特别强调恬淡虚无，精神内守，而养生功正是贯穿这些要求的。紧张、繁忙、快节奏的现代都市生活，给人们带来精神紧张、情绪烦躁、思维紊乱等负效应，甚至影响身体健康，降低工作效率。养生功要求清静无为，通过自我意念控制，使身体和精神获得最大限度的放松，以缓解精神紧张和压力，使情感活动趋于平和稳定，减少致病的内在因素，从而提高健康水平。

2. Adjusting the structure of bones, joints and muscles, improving the ability of physical exercise

Through the movement method of twisting and screwing, The exercise produces a reasonable physiological burden, which will make bones, joints and muscles gain systematical and all-sided training, and further make bone thicker, increase the bone's diameter, make the tuber appending to muscles in the surface of bones distinct, and making the array of bone trabecula more orderly and regular. These changes can strengthen the metabolism of bones, and produce good effects in forms and structures. With the changes of forms and structures, bones will become firmer and firmer, and the capabilities of bones such as anti-folding, anti-pressing, anti-twisting etc, will also be improved.

The twisting and screwing relaxant movement of the exercise

can make dense bones in the surface of joints thicker, tendon and ligament stronger, diameters of appending points of bones wider, ossein contents richer, joint cartilages thicker, and quantities of cell nuclei per unit volume increasing. In addition to increasing muscle's strength, it can make joints of bones firmer, sinews and ligaments around joint antrums more flexible, and further increase the movement range of joints. Therefore people who often practice the exercise will not only have good flexibility, but also lay a foundation for fighting and defending.

Through wresting repeatedly, cooperated with relaxation consciously, screwy twisting movement can make all parts of our body take part in actions, and make muscle fibers extend to a degree that normal movement cannot reach. With practicing, the quantities of bioblast in muscle fibers increases, the volume becomes larger, the fat in muscles becomes less, the connective tissue becomes more, and the attending muscle fibers and capillary vessels increase. Therefore the skin of people who often practice the exercise will become smooth and light, and their muscles will have good flexibility, strong and handsome. The exercise can improve the stature of people who are too thin or too fat when practicing the exercise.

The process of relaxing brain and relaxing sporting body together, will improve the controlling course of nerve, and at the same time the consuming energy during movement will be decreased and ATP will be deposited into muscles. Because of the increase of ATP deposit in muscles, the speed of ATP decomposing and recomposing is increased. Therefore it strengthens people's ability of quick reaction and quick movement, makes people grasp the keys of the actions quickly and increase their athletic technical level.

二、改善骨骼、关节和肌肉的结构，提高运动能力

养生功以缠绕螺旋的运动方式，产生合理的生理负荷，使骨骼、关节、肌肉得到系统全面的锻炼，如使骨密质增厚，骨径变粗，骨面肌附着处突起明显，骨小梁的排列更加整齐规律等。这些变化会增强骨的新陈代谢，在形态结构上产生良好效果。随着形态结构的变化，骨变得更加坚固，从而提高了抗折、抗压、抗扭转等性能。

养生功这种放松性缠绕螺旋运动，可使关节面骨密质增厚，肌腱和韧带增粗，在骨附着处直径增大，胶原含量增加，关节软骨增厚，单位体积内细胞核数目增多，再加上肌肉力量的增强，就加大了关节的稳固性，以及关节囊周围肌腱、韧带的延展性，从而使关节活动幅度增大。因而，经常练养生功的人不仅柔韧性好，还能为进一步学习擒拿与反擒拿奠定良好基础。

螺旋式的缠绕运动，通过反复拧转绞动，配合有意识的放松放长，可使全身各部都参加活动，使肌纤维拉长到一般运动难以达到的长度。锻炼日久，肌纤维中线粒体数目增多，体积增大，肌肉中脂肪减少，结缔组织增多，参与活动的肌纤维和毛细血管数量增加。因而，经常练养生功的人皮肤会逐渐变得细腻光泽，肌肉弹性好，健美有力。过瘦、过胖的人练习养生功后，体型都会有明显改善。

大脑放松入静与身体放松运动相结合,改善了神经控制过程,同时也减少了运动过程中的能量损耗,使 ATP 储存于肌肉中。由于肌肉中 ATP 含量的增加,加快了在神经冲动作用下 ATP 的分解和再合成速度,因而加强了人体的快速反应、快速运动能力,能较快地掌握动作要领,提高运动技术水平。

3. Strengthening the digestive system, improving the respiration functions

The digestive system consists of digestive glands and enteron. Its basic functions are to ingest food, digest food, absorb nutrition and obviate draff. It is related to the functions of various organs whether the person is healthy or not. The actions of the exercise are mild and slow. With the actions, the internal energy gets through the viscera and antrum. Deep and long breath also makes the midriff muscles move up and down in a wild range, and the abdomen muscles move greatly, which forms benign massage to intestines and stomachs. At this time digestive glands perspire more digestive secretion, and therefore the period of digestion will be shortened, and absorption of nutritions becomes more favorably. Hence practicing the exercise can improve the appetite, and strengthen the digestive ability. This will be good for curing dyspepsia, gastrointestinal neurosis and gastric ulcer, etc.

The exercise requires that actions and breath should cooperate with each other. If so, the energy will get through all limbs, the breath will also change from quickness to slowness, and then become deep and long. During such a process, the contractive and spreading abilities of midriff muscles will be improved, the traction force between thoraxes strengthened, the contacting area between capillary vessels and alveoluses enlarged, and the vital capacity improved. If you keep on persistently practising, the vital capacity will be improved distinctly, and breath and actions will cooperate more in phase. So you can keep continually working for a long time without tiredness. Practising the exercise can not only prevent chronic diseases, but also improve working efficiency greatly.

三、锻炼消化系统,增强呼吸机能

消化系统由消化道和消化腺组成,它的基本功能是摄取食物、消化食物、吸收营养物质和排泄残渣。人体健康与否,与消化系统各器官的功能关系密切。养生功动作柔和缓慢,随着动作导引,内气贯通五脏六腑。深长的腹式呼吸,也使膈肌大幅度地上下移动和腹肌大量活动,形成了对肠胃器官的良性按摩。此时,消化腺分泌的消化液增多,缩短了消化时间,使营养物质的吸收更加顺畅。所以练习养生功能够增强食欲,提高消化能力,有助于消化不良、胃肠官能症及溃疡等疾病的治疗。

养生功要求动作与呼吸密切配合,气贯四梢,必然使呼吸由快变慢,逐渐深长,使膈肌的收缩和舒张能力提高,胸廓间的牵张力加大,肺泡与毛细血管壁的接触面积增加,肺活量逐渐增大。持久练习,肺通气量和最大吸气量都会明显增加,呼吸与动作配合更加协调。这样，在定量工作时，能保持较长时间连续工作而工作能力不致下降。所以，练养生功不仅能防治慢性肺病，还能大大提高工作实效。

4. Strengthening the functions of heart, improving the working ability of vessel system

Persisting in the exercise can make the cardiac muscle fibers wider, the wall of heart thicker, the contracting ability better, the content of heart and send out per pulse increasing. In addition, it can improve the flexibility and tenacity of arterial wall, make the diameter of coronary arteries wider. These changes make vessel system complete, and make nutrition absorbed by digestive organs, oxygen absorbed by lungs and hormone perspired by internal secretory glands be carried to varieties of organs and tissues. Therefore it will be beneficial to metabolism and stability of the internal circumstances. A person who exercises insistently, will own a stronger heart. The rate of heart beating is slow, when you are quiet; increasing a little when you moving normally; and much increasing but quick resuming in when vividly moving.

四、增强心脏功能，改善脉管系统的工作能力

通过持久的养生功锻炼，可使心肌纤维增粗，心壁增厚，心脏收缩力增强，心脏的容量及每搏输出量增加。此外，还能改善

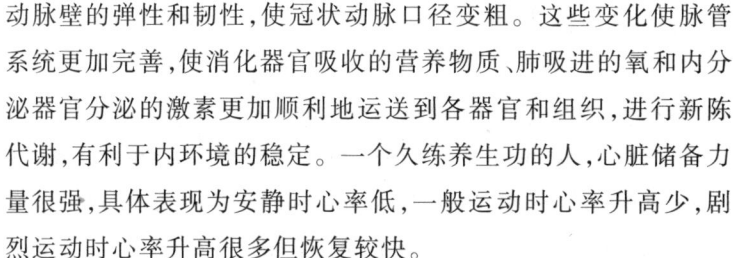

动脉壁的弹性和韧性，使冠状动脉口径变粗。这些变化使脉管系统更加完善，使消化器官吸收的营养物质、肺吸进的氧和内分泌器官分泌的激素更加顺利地运送到各器官和组织，进行新陈代谢，有利于内环境的稳定。一个久练养生功的人，心脏储备力量很强，具体表现为安静时心率低，一般运动时心率升高少，剧烈运动时心率升高很多但恢复较快。

5. Stimulating the internal energy, smoothing the Jingluo

Jingluo are the main channels where people's energy running through. These channels of jingluo are related with people's pathological and physiological causes. Smooth channels will make bodies healthy, whereas jammed channels induce diseases. Therefore 《Lingshu · Jingbie》says: "the twelve channels are the cause of people's living, the cause of diseases, the beginning of learning, and the ending of working." And it also says, "Therefore deciding living and death, dispelling all diseases, concocting the false vigor and the real energy, all rely on smooth channels." Although the methods of practising breath exercises vary in some way, their basic aims are to get enough internal energy, and lead the internal energy through the twelve channels, big and small Zhoutian points, and therefore reach the aim of preventing and curing diseases, strengthening body, benefiting wisdom and life.

The internal vital energy is a kind of living energy current inside human body. Its intensity is decided by the health degree of human body. Although it is accompanied with life, its flourish and declination cannot be detached from the postnatal culture. As long as the exercising method is reasonable, the internal energy can be assembled and strengthened. Then you can use the large internal energy to strengthen body, protect body from enemies. With special method, the exercise adopts a reasonable posture leading human vigor to assemble, complete, enrich, strengthen and sway, and get through the twelve regular channels and eight extraordinary channels, enriching all the body. Under the lead of will, when the internal energy goes through heart, the irritation in your heart will become weak, the kidney fluid will become warm. When it going through the lungs, the lung's energy will fall into the kidney, and deposit in Dantian. When I going through liver, the irritation in your will become mild, the brain will become clear, and the eyes will become bright. When it going through spleens, it will bring health and postnatal energy, and your skins will become smooth and bright. When it going through vessels, there will not be stymies. When it going through the hair, your sense will become sensitive. It likes as the specialists of health-preserving say: "Using my heart and energy onto my body to cure my diseases. How couldn't the diseases be cured?"

五、鼓荡内气，畅通经络

经络是人体气血运行的通道，与人的生理病理关系密切。经络畅通则身体健康，经络不通则生疾病。所以《灵枢·经别》篇："夫十二经脉者，人之所以生，病之所以成，人之所以治，病之所以起，学之所始，工之所止也。"又云"所以决生死，去百病，调虚实，不可不通"。气功锻炼的方式、途径虽不尽相同，但根本目的都在于练就充足的内气，并运用内气贯通十二经脉、奇经八脉，通大小周天，从而达到防病治病、强健身体，益智延年的目的。

内气是人体内的生命能量流，其强弱决定人体的健康程度，虽然内气与生俱来，但其盛衰却离不开后天的培养，只要锻炼方法科学、合理，就能使内气汇聚和增强，进而利用这充沛强大的内气增强体质，防身御敌，这里养生功以它特有的方式，在安逸清静的意识支配下，通过合理的姿势导引使人体自身具有的先天之气在短时间内汇聚、饱满、充实、壮大、鼓荡，渐渐贯通十二正经、奇经八脉，充实全身。在意识的引导下，内气行于心，则心火不亢，肾水不寒；内气行于肺，则升降自如，肺气下纳于肾，气沉丹田，运动而不气喘；内气行于肝，则肝火得平，脑清目明；内气行于脾，则运化得健，后天之本生机旺盛，肌肤健美光泽；内气行于血脉之间，则营卫无滞；内气行于肌肤毫毛，则感觉灵敏，梢节充足。正如养生家言："以我之心，使我之气，适我之体，攻我之疾，何往而不愈焉？"

Section III The Main Points and Detailed Request of Exercising

第三节 练功要领及具体要求

1. Easy and quiet, natural and yielding

To be easy aims at forms, not only the muscles but also the bones, internal organs, skins and hair must relax. Every part of the body should not have any tensity. To be quiet aims at will. The mind must be assembled peacefully when exercising intently, and you should obviate all useless thoughts. Being intent can bring good effects. To be natural means not holding back breath and not using stiff power. The actions should cooperate with breath naturally without any suppression.

一、松静安逸，自然顺遂

松，指形体而言，不但肌肉要放松，连同骨骼、内脏、皮肤、毛发都要松，全身各处无丝毫紧张感。静，指意念而言，思想清静集中，排除一切杂念，专心练功。练功时一定要放下任何杂务，一心一意，才会取得良好功效。自然，这里也指练功时不憋气，

不用僵力，动作与呼吸配合听任自然，毫不勉强。

2. Energy following will, forms integrating with spirit to one

Let the will lead energy. Cooperate actions with breath tightly. When the will reaches, the energy and strength shall follow. The normal rule of the cooperation between actions and breath in movement exercises is to combine inhaling with exhaling, inducing inhaling to exhaling, inhaling when ascending and exhaling when descending, inhaling when saving energy, exhaling when sending out energy. In a word, you must obey the nature. You should not deliberately make your breath longer just for cooperating with the actions, or you will be blocked in breathing and become idiotic.

二、意气相随，形神合一

以意领气，动作与呼吸密切配合，意到、气到、劲到。动功中动作与呼吸配合的一般规律是：合吸开呼，引吸放呼；上升吸气，下降呼气；蓄劲吸气，发劲呼气等等。总之，要任其自然，不可为了配合动作故意拉长呼吸，导致呼吸不畅，神气呆滞。

3. Staying upright and middle, discriminating from the emptiness and the solidity

In both practising movement exercises and practising quiet exercises, require your body to keep staying upright, middle and not slanting. You should not sway right or left, incline east and west. The detailed methods of actions are to keep naturally head right, neck and shoulder relaxed, elbows declined, chest cherished and waist sinking. When your body moves, your head and neck must be consistent with your four limbs, your two eyes should look forward flatly, the points of Baihui and Changqiang should concentrate on each other. When pratising, you must carefully taste the transferring of the gravity of body, discriminate from the negative and the positive, the false and the actual. And you must taste seriously whether the route of energy or the actions are smooth, and should regulate them immediately when false. You must obey the rule of being still rather than movement, and must pay attention to the holistic cooperation of hands, eyes, posture and steps in perfect harmony and spirit, vigor, soul, power and exercise in the same direction. In a word, you must obey the rules without any carelessness.

三、立身中正,分清虚实

不论练动功还是练静功,都要求立身中正,不偏不倚。不可左右摇晃，东倒西歪。具体做法是：头自然正，颈项松，松肩，沉肘，含胸，塌腰。身体移动和旋转时，头颈部与身躯四肢要上下一致，两眼平视，百会穴与长强穴相互贯注。在练功过程中，要仔细体会重心的转移，分清阴阳虚实，认真体会劲路是否畅通，动作是否顺遂，不符合要求时立即调整。练功时要贯穿一动无有不动的练功原则，注意整体配合，做到手、眼、身法、步协调一致，精、气、神、力、功专注一方，循规蹈矩，一丝不苟。

4. Practising time and movement amount

The time for practising the exercise should be from 20 minutes to 1 hour every time. And more practicing, more time should be spent, increasing gradually. The amount of activity should be arranged in accordance with different personal situation. It is suitable for a healthy person if he feels a little fatigue and refreshment after practising the exercise. The weak should put more emphasis on the quiet exercise, and make his posture higher when practising the movement exercise, and then lower his posture gradually after his body becomes stronger. The strong may emphasize the movement exercise, with posture lower.

四、练功时间及运动量

练功时间每次 20 分钟至 1 小时，逐渐增加。运动量要根据个人身体素质灵活安排，健康者以练完后身体稍感疲劳但精神舒畅为适宜。体弱者可侧重练静功,练动功时架式适当放高,待身体强壮再慢慢降低身法;体质强壮者可侧重动功练习,身法下低。

Attention:

The patient should not feel too much fatigue. As soon as he feels fatigue, he should have a rest immediately, and then go on to practise it when he is renewed, in order to avoid making the disease more serious.

注意:

病患者练功不宜过于疲劳,一感到疲劳,就应立即休息,待体力恢复后再继续练,以免加重病情。

Chapter Two The Basic Training

第二章 基本功训练

Section I The Exercise of Joint Movement

第一节 关节活动操

In human body, the blood is attributed to the Yin, the energy is attributed to the Yang. The blood is the mother of energy, and the energy is the leader of blood. Blood follows the energy. Through actions of the joints such as joint between shoulder and arm, joint between waist and stern, knee joint, elbow joint, wrist joint and ankles joint, the movement exercise of joints makes muscles and tendons loosened, the joints stretched, the vein smooth to promote the walking of blood and the energy. The movement exercise of joints is preparative actions before exercising. They can inspire the spirit and strengthen the exercising effect. If you practise it alone, it may smooth your channels, prevent you from arthritis.

The preparative actions should not be too much. It should be finished when your body sweating slightly, not when you have been gasping.

在人体中，血属阴，气属阳，血为气之母，气为血之帅，血随气行。通过肩臂、腰胯、膝、肘、腕、踝等关节活动，使肌肉、筋腱松弛，关节舒展，血脉畅通，促进气血运行。关节活动操作为正式练功前的准备活动，可以振奋精神，强化练功效果；若单独操练，可舒筋活络，防治关节炎。

准备活动不宜过多，以身体微微出汗而不气喘为宜。

1. Swaying head

Fig. 2-1

Fig. 2-2

Fig. 2-3

Stand upright naturally with feet about shoulder-width apart. Place the both hands on the sides of the waist with the thumbs in the rear and the other fingers at front. Then, using the neck as the pivot, sway the head leftward, backward, rightward, forward and leftward in a circle for eight times. And then sway the head for eight times in the reverse direction (Fig. 2-1、2-2、2-3).

一、旋转头颈

两脚自然开立,约与肩同宽。双手叉腰,拇指在后,其余四指在前。以颈项为轴,头向左→向后→向右→向前→向左旋转为1圈,共转8圈,再反方向旋转8圈(图2-1、2-2、2-3)。

2. Wrist exercise

Stand upright naturally with feet about shoulder-width apart. Join your hands in front of the body with the fingers interlaced. Then, using the wrist as the pivot, sway the fingers gently many times, the amplitude of rotation should as large as possible (Fig. 2-4).

Fig. 2-4

二、活动腕关节

两脚自然开立,约与肩同宽。两手十指环扣交叉于胸前。以腕关节为轴旋转,动作尽量轻柔,幅度要大,次数不限,以舒适为度(图2-4)。

3. Elbow exercise

Stand upright naturally with feet about shoulder-width apart. Hang arms down at the thighs. Move the arms outward, forward and upward in arcs, and close them to in the front of abdomen, while the arms changing from adverse twining to smooth twining (Fig. 2-5). Without stopping previous movement. Move the both hands inward, downward and outward in arcs passing to the sides of thighs (Fig. 2-6). Repeat the previous movement many times.

Fig. 2-5

Fig. 2-6

三、活动肘关节

两脚自然开立,约与肩同宽。两手臂自然垂于体侧。以身体带动手臂先逆缠进而变顺缠走外前上弧形合于腹前(图 2-5)。上动不停,双手变逆缠走里下弧循腰两侧外开至两胯侧(图 2-6)。反复练习。

4. Shoulder exercise

Fig. 2-7

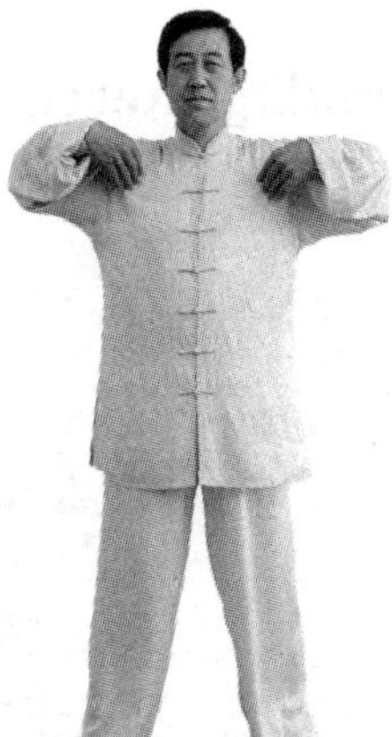

Fig. 2-8

Fig. 2-9

Stand upright naturally with feet about shoulder-width apart. Change the both hands into hook-hands and then place them in the front of the shoulders. Then, using the shoulders joints as pivots, move the both elbows forward, upward, backward and downward in circles, do eight circles (Fig. 2-7、2-8、2-9). And then do these exercises eight times in the adverse direction. Repeat these movements many times.

四、活动肩关节

两脚自然开立,约与肩同宽。双手成勾手,勾尖置于肩前。以肩关节为轴,两肘向前→向上→向后→向下旋转为1圈,共转8圈(图2-7、2-8、2-9),再反方向旋转8圈。反复练习。

5. Chest-expanding exercise

Fig. 2-10

Fig. 2-11

Stand upright naturally with feet about shoulder-width apart. Raise both hands horizontally in front of chest with the palms facing downward and fingers pointing each other. And then stretch both elbows vigorously to the sides and backs of body (Fig. 2-10). Return to starting position and stretch arms vigorously to the sides and backs of body with the palms facing upward (Fig. 2-11). Repeat these movements many times.

五、扩胸

两脚自然开立,约与肩同宽。双手平抬于胸前,掌心向下,指尖相对。两脚不动,两肘外张扩胸(图 2-10)。随两臂回弹,两臂成侧平举扩胸,掌心朝上(图 2-11)。反复练习。

6. Arms swing exercise

Stand upright naturally with feet about shoulder-width apart. Raise the left hand to the upward-left of the head with the arm straight and the palm facing forward, place the right hand on the right side of the body. And then swing both arms backward for four times (Fig. 2-12). Change the upper and lower positions of the hands and swing them backward four times. (Fig. 2-13). Repeat these movements many times.

Fig. 2-12

Fig. 2-13

六、振臂

两脚自然开立，约与肩同宽。左手上举于头部左侧，臂伸直，掌心朝前，右臂垂于右侧。两臂同时后振 4 次(图 2-12)，再交换两手上下位置，后振 4 次(图 2-13)。反复练习。

7. Patting exercise

Stand upright naturally with feet about shoulder-width apart. The shoulders, arms and hips are relaxed, the knees bent slightly. Fix the both feet and turn the body to the left. Following the turning of the body, swing the both arms to pat the body, using the right arm to pat the left side of chest, abdomen, rib and shoulder, using the back of left hand and left forearm to pat the right side of back. Eyes look the rear-left of body (Fig. 2-14). And then do these movements in the sever direction (Fig. 2-15). Such as repeat previous movements, the times are not limited.

Fig. 2-14

Fig. 2-15

七、抡臂拍打

两脚自然开立,约与肩同宽。松肩、松臂、松胯、屈膝。脚不动,随着身体左转,带动两臂甩开拍打身体。右臂拍打左前胸、腹、肋、肩,左手背及前臂拍打右背,眼随身体向左后方看(图 2-14)。再向右转,动作相同,方向相反(图 2-15)。如此自下而上、自上而下随意拍打,次数不限,以轻松舒适为度。

8. Twisting waist

Stand upright naturally with feet about shoulder-width apart. Clench the hands into fists and raise them horizontally in the front of the chest with the faces of fists facing each other. The feet do not move. Twist the waist leftward 90 degrees for two times (Fig. 2-16). And then twist waist rightward 90 degrees for two times (2-17). Repeat these movements.

Fig. 2-16

Fig. 2-17

八、转腰

两脚自然开立，约与肩同宽。双手轻握拳，平抬与胸平，拳面相对。脚不动,向左转腰 90 度 2 次(图 2-16),随即向右转腰 90 度 2 次(图 2-17)。反复练习。

9. Hips exercise

Stand upright naturally with feet about shoulder-width apart. Place both hands on sides of waist with the thumbs in the front and the other four fingers on the "shenshu" (Fig. 2-18). Using the joints of hips as pivots, move the hips leftward, backward, rightward and forward for eight circles (Fig. 2-19、2-20). Then change the direction and repeat these movements.

Fig. 2-18

Fig. 2-19

Fig. 2-20

九、活动髋关节

两脚自然开立，约与肩同宽。两手虎口叉腰（图 2-18），拇指在前，其余 4 指按于肾俞穴上。腰不动，以髋关节为轴。按左→后→右→前的方向旋转 8 圈（图 2-19、2-20），再反方向旋转 8 圈。反复练习。

10. Knees exercise

Fig. 2-21

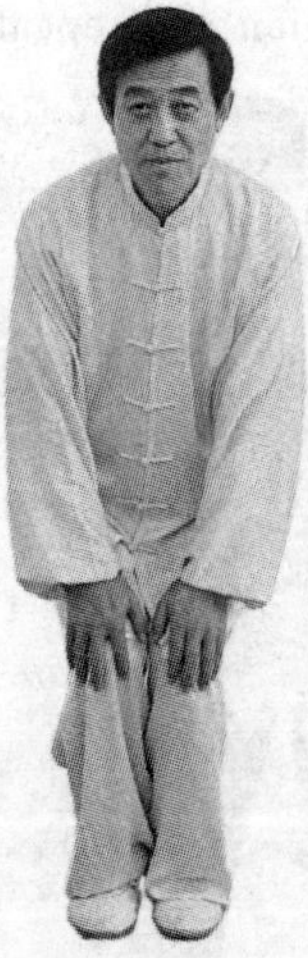

Fig. 2-22

Stand upright naturally with feet about shoulder-width apart. Press the both palms on the knees, using the kneecaps as pivots, move the knees inward, backward, outward and inward for eight circles (Fig. 2-21). Place the both feet together, the postures of palms are not changed, using the knees as pivots, move to the left and the right respective sides eight circles (Fig. 2-22). Repeat these movements.

十、活动膝关节

两脚自然开立,约与肩同宽。两手掌按在膝盖上,以膝关节为轴。同时向里、向外各旋转 8 圈(图 2-21)。两脚并拢,手势不变,以膝关节为轴,向左、向右各旋转 8 圈(图 2-22)。反复练习。

11. Ankles exercise

Stand upright naturally. Place the both hands on the sides of waist with the thumbs in the rear and the other four fingers at the front. Shift the weight on the right leg, the toes of left foot landing on the floor. Using the toes of left foot as a supporting point and the ankle joint as an axis, move the ankle in the circle line (Fig. 2-23). And then using the toes of right foot as a supporting point, move the right ankle joint (Fig. 2-24). Repeat these movements.

Fig. 2-23

Fig. 2-24

十一、活动踝关节

两脚自然站立。双手叉腰,拇指在后,其余4指在前,重心在右腿,左脚点地。右脚不动,以左脚尖为支点,以左踝关节为轴旋转(图2-23),再以右脚尖点地,旋转右踝关节(图2-24)。反复练习。

12. Relaxing exercise

Stand at attention. Shift the weight on the right leg and lift the left foot, relax hips and bend knees, withdraw the arms, turn the body to the right slightly (Fig. 2-25). Kick downward with the left foot and throw the both arms downward, relax the joints of entire body (Fig. 2-26). Then change the right foot, the movements are same, the direction is adverse (Fig. 2-27、2-28).

Fig. 2-25

Fig. 2-26

Fig. 2-27

Fig. 2-28

十二、弹抖放松

立正。左脚提起,右腿支撑体重,松胯屈膝,两臂放松收缩,身体略右转(图 2-25)。放松弹蹬左脚,同时向右前下甩两手臂,全身各个关节都有一种放松舒展的感觉(图 2-26);换提右脚弹抖放松,动作相同,方向相反(图 2-27、2-28)。

Section II Training of Twining Power
第二节 缠丝劲训练

1. Wave the single hand

1) Wave the left hand

① Both legs form a bow stance. The center of gravity is on the left leg. Ward off the left palm to in the upside of the left knee, at the shoulder level. Place the right palm on the right side of the waist with the thumb behind and the other fingers in front. Eyes look the left hand (Fig. 2-29).

② Continuing from the previous movement. The body turns to the right, the center of gravity moves to the right leg. At the same time, move the left palm downward and rightward in an arc to in the front of abdomen. It is called "smooth twining power" (Fig. 2-30).

Fig. 2-29

Fig. 2-30

③ Continuing from the previous movement. Continue to turn the body to the right. At the same time, threat the left palm right-ward and upward to in the right side of the front of the chest with the palm turning outward, it is called "adverse twining power". Eyes look to forward-right (Fig. 2-31).

④ Continuing from the previous movement. Relax the left hip, turn the body to the left, move the left upward and leftward in an arc to the upside of the left knee, at the shoulder level. Eyes look at the left palm (Fig. 2-32). In this way, an opening and a closing form a beat. Exercise the single movement, should be finish sixteen beats to form a division. The beginners must grasp the line of the movement first, and then realize the moving of the weight, turning of the waist and changes of twining of arms. In this way, from harsh to skilled, from skilled to smooth, achieve progressively the coordination of the all body and consistent of the power. When grasping movements well, coordinate with the breathe in the movements, exhale in the opening power with adverse twining, internal power flows from the Dantian to the fingers; inhale in the closing power with smooth twining, collect the fresh air from the center of palm to Dantian.

Fig. 2-31

Fig. 2-32

(2) Wave the right hand

The essential points are the same as described in the previous exercise Wave the Right Hand, reversing left and right (Fig. 2-33、2-34、2-35、2-36).

Fig. 2-33

Fig. 2-34

Fig. 2-35

Fig. 2-36

一、单云手

1. 左单云手

动作一:两脚开步成左弓步,左手上掤至左膝上方与肩平;右手叉腰,拇指在后,其余4指在前,目视左手,重心在左(图2-29)。

动作二:接上势,身体向右转,重心移至右腿;同时左手划弧下沉,里合于小腹前,为顺缠丝劲(图2-30)。

动作三:接上势,身体继续右转,同时左手向右上穿掌外翻至右胸前,为逆缠丝劲。目视身体右侧前方(图2-31)。

动作四:接上势,松左胯,身体左转,左手逆缠外开至左膝方与肩平,目视左手(图2-32)。如此整个左单云手动作完成。一开一合为1拍,一般在每个动作单练时,练够两个8拍为1节。初学者先搞清楚动作的路线,熟练后,再体会重心移动的盘旋路线,以及腰左右旋转和手臂顺逆缠丝的转换速度。只有这样,才能由生到熟,由熟到顺,逐步达到周身相随,连绵不断。动作特别熟练后,再配合呼吸。开劲逆缠时呼气,内气由丹田催达手指;合劲顺缠时吸气,采自然界清灵之气由掌心顺缠收于丹田之内,充实丹田。

2. 右单云手

动作要领与左单云手相同,方向相反(图2-33、2-34、2-35、2-36)。

2. Wave the both hands

Fig. 2-37

Fig. 2-38

(1) From the Wave the Left Hand (Fig. 2-32), turn the body to the left slightly, move the right palm downward and leftward in an arc from the side of the waist to in the front of the abdomen with smooth twining, ward off the left palm upward with adverse twining. Eyes look to forward-right (Fig. 2-37).

(2) Continuing from the previous movement. Turn the body first to the left and then to the right, the center of gravity moves to the right leg. At the same time, move the right palm leftward and upward, and then rightward and upward with adverse twining. Move the left palm downward and inward to in the front of the abdomen. Eyes look to forward-left (Fig. 2-38). In the way, exercise the pre-

vious movements circulate so the turning of body and twining of both arms are coordinated.

二、双云手

动作一:由左单云手(图 2-32)起势,身体微左转,右手由右腰间顺缠划弧下沉于小腹前;左手变逆缠上挪,目视右前方(图 2-37)。

动作二:接上势,身体先左后右转,重心由左腿移至右腿;同时右手向左向上,变逆缠向右上挪,左手划弧顺缠里合于小腹前,目视左前方(图 2-38)。这样反复循环运转,练习旋转腰,两臂左右缠丝,周身协调一致。

3. Wave the hand in the side of body

Fig. 2-39

Fig. 2-40

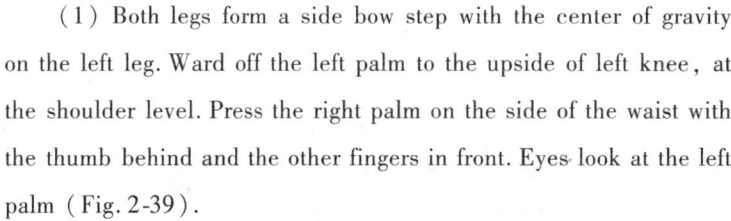

(1) Both legs form a side bow step with the center of gravity on the left leg. Ward off the left palm to the upside of left knee, at the shoulder level. Press the right palm on the side of the waist with the thumb behind and the other fingers in front. Eyes look at the left palm (Fig. 2-39).

(2) Continuing from the previous movement. Turn the body to the left, move the left palm outward in an arc to in the rear-left of body. Eyes look at the left palm (Fig. 2-40).

(3) Turn the body to the right, move the center of gravity to the right leg. Move the left palm downward and forward to in the upside of the left knee. Eyes look to lower-front (Fig. 2-41).

Fig. 2-41

Fig. 2-42

(4) Turn the body to the left slightly. Move the left palm upward with adverse twining to the upside of left knee (Fig. 2-42). An opening and a closing form a beat, exercise the previous movements

sixteen beats. And then do right palm exercise, The essential points are the same as described in the previous exercise, reversing left and right (Fig. 2-43、2-44、2-45、2-46).

Fig. 2-43

Fig. 2-44

Fig. 2-45

Fig. 2-46

三、侧面缠丝

动作一：两脚横开成左弓步，左手掤至左膝上与肩平；右手叉腰，拇指在后，其余 4 指在前，重心在左，眼看左手（图 2-39）。

动作二：接上势，身体左转，左手逆缠划弧外开至身体左侧后方，眼看左手（图 2-40）。

动作三：身体右转，重心移至右腿，左手顺缠里合于左膝上方，眼顺左手看左前下方（图 2-41）。

动作四：身体略左转，左手逆缠上掤至左膝上方（图 2-42）。一开一合为 1 拍，共练两个 8 拍。再换右手练习，动作要领相同，唯左右互换（图 2-43、2-44、2-45、2-46）。

4. Deflect backward in both sides of body

(1) Both legs form a right bow step. Place the left palm in the front of chest, at the shoulder level. Close the right palm on the side of waist. Eyes look forward (Fig. 2-47).

(2) Continuing from the previous movement. Turn the body to the left slightly, move the weight to the left leg. At the same time, deflect the left palm downward and backward to the side of waist with adverse twining, deflect the right palm backward with adverse twining first and then move it to in the forward-right of body with smooth twining. Eyes look forward (Fig. 2-48). In the way, exercising the previous movements circulate, pay attention to that the

waist serves as an axis to initiate the movements of the arms, the waist initiating the shoulder, the shoulders initiating elbows, at the last reach the hands. When changing the deflecting of the palm backward into the raising upward, don't shrug the shoulders.

Fig. 2-47

Fig. 2-48

四、左右后捋

动作一：两腿成右弓步，左手置于胸前与肩平；右手合于右腰间，目视前方（图2-47）。

动作二：接上势，身体微左转，重心移至左腿；同时左手逆缠下捋至腰间，右手先逆缠后捋变顺缠上翻至身体右前方，目视前方（图2-48）。这样循环往返，反复练习，以身领手，以腰催肩，以肩催肘，再达手，练习周身结合的后捋劲。注意：在后捋转折上翻时,切勿挑肩。

5. Twining both hands

(1) Stand upright with feet together, and then lift the left foot take a step forward, ward off the both palms forward, upward in arcs and deflect them backward, the left hand twining smoothly and the right hand twining adversely. Eyes look forward (Fig. 2-49).

(2) Continuing from the previous movement. Turn the body to the right, deflect the both palms backward, move the weight to the left (Fig. 2-50).

Fig. 2-49

Fig. 2-50

(3) Continuing from the previous movement. Turn the body to

the left, ward off the both palms in downward and forward arcs with the left arm twining adversely and the right arm twining smoothly. The weight is on the left leg (Fig. 2-51).

Fig. 2-51

Fig. 2-52

(4) Continuing from the previous movement. Turn the body to the right, deflect the both palms backward with the right arm twining adversely and the left arm twining smoothly (Fig. 2-52).

Repeat the previous exercise, can change it to the left or right. Pay attention to that the waist serves as an axis to initiate the movements of the arms, use the will to initiate the energy.

五、前后双手缠丝

动作一:先立正成预备姿势,然后提左腿向前上步,两手左顺右逆缠丝,向前划弧上掤后攌,目视前方(图 2-49)。

动作二:接上势,身体右转,两手后攌,重心左移(图 2-50)。

动作三:接上势,身体左转,两手走下弧左逆右顺缠向前掤,重心在左腿(图 2-51)。

动作四:接上势,身体右转,两手右逆左顺缠向上后攌(图 2-52)。

反复练习以上动作,也可右腿在前,左腿在后,左右调换。以裆腰为轴旋转,带动两臂缠丝,以身领手,以意导气。

Section III Stance Training Methods
第三节 步法训练

1. Forward step

(1) Stand upright with feet together. The body relaxed and concentration settling to Dantian. Eyes look forward (Fig. 2-53).

(2) Continuing from the previous movement. Shift the weight to the left leg, lift the left leg and take a step to the forward-left with the left foot. At the same time, move the both palms in forward and upward arcs, and then deflect them backward, the left arm twining smoothly and the right arm twining adversely. Eyes look forward (Fig. 2-54).

(3) Continuing from the previous movement. Shift the weight

to the left leg, withdraw the right foot to the inside of the left foot. At the same time, ward off the both palms downward and forward with the left arm twining adversely and right arm twining smoothly. Eyes look forward (Fig. 2-55). And then take a step forward with left foot and deflect the both palms backward, repeat the previous movement (Fig. 2-54), so that the movements of the hands are well-coordinated with the foot. Such as do the exercise several times, then do the right symmetrical exercise, take a step with the right foot and withdraw the left foot, the essential points are same as the previous movement.

Fig. 2-53

Fig. 2-54

Fig. 2-55

一、前进步

动作一：立正。周身放松，意守丹田，目视前方（图 2-53）。

动作二：接上势，重心移至右腿，提左腿向左前方上步，两手同时自下而上左顺右逆向前上划弧后掤，目视前方（图 2-54）。

动作三：接上势，重心移至左腿，右脚跟步与左脚并齐；同时双手变左逆右顺缠走下弧向前掤，目视前方（图 2-55）。然后再上步后掤，如图 2-54 所示，以练习手脚配合，周身相随。这样反复练习若干次后，换右脚上步，左脚跟步练习，要领同上。

2. Backward step

(1) Stand upright with feet together. Eyes look forward. Close the right palm to the right side of waist and push the left palm forward with the center of the palm facing forward, the elbow lowered and the shoulders relaxed (Fig. 2-56).

(2) Continuing from the previous movement. Shift the center of gravity to the right leg, the left foot steps in an arc to the rear-left past the inside of the right foot, the ball of the left foot sliding on the floor. At the same time, following the stepping backward of the left foot, deflect the left palm downward and backward in an arc with the arm twining adversely, move the right palm backward and upward and then push it forward (Fig. 2-57).

Fig. 2-56

Fig. 2-57

(3) Continuing from the previous movement. Shift the weight to the left leg, the right foot steps in an arc to the rear-right past the inside of the left foot, the ball of the right foot sliding on the floor. At the same time, following the stepping backward of the right foot, deflect the right palm downward and backward in an arc with the arm twining adversely, move the left palm backward and upward and then push it forward (Fig. 2-58).

Fig. 2-58

The movements are methods of training the coordination of upper and lower limbs in stepping backward. Repeat it in the same way.

二、后退步

动作一:两脚并立,目视前方。右手合于右腰间,左手手心朝前推出,沉肘松肩(图 2-56)。

动作二:接上势,重心移至右腿,提左腿,脚尖着地,向内划弧后退;同时左手逆缠向下划弧随左腿后摆,右手由后上翻前推(图 2-57)。

动作三:接上势,重心移至左腿,提右腿,脚尖着地,向内侧划弧后退;同时右手逆缠向下划弧随右腿后摆,左手由后上翻前推(图 2-58)。

此动作是练习退步时上下配合的方法,可反复练习,练习次数根据场地灵活掌握。

3. Side step

(1) Stand upright with feet together. Press the right palm on the side of the waist with the thumb behind and the other fingers in front. Move the left palm to the left side of the body with the center of palm facing leftward, the shoulder relaxed and the elbow lowered. Eyes look forward (Fig. 2-59).

(2) Continuing from the previous movement. Turn the body slightly to the right, shift the weight to the right leg, lift the left leg and take a step leftward with the left foot. At the same time, move

the left palm downward and rightward in an arc with the arm twining smoothly. Eyes look to forward-left (Fig. 2-60).

Fig. 2-59

Fig. 2-60

(3) Continuing from the previous movement. Turn the body slightly to the left, shift the weight to the left leg, lift the right leg and withdraw the right foot to the inside of the left foot. At the same time, move the left palm inward and upward and leftward in an arc with the arm twining adversely. Eyes look to the forward-left (Fig. 2-61).

The posture is method of training the closing of hand and opening of foot, the opening of hand and closing of foot or the leading of the upper limbs and the advancing of lower limbs. Repeat the previous exercise. And then take a step rightward, the essential points are the same as described in the previous exercise, reversing left and right (Fig. 2-62, 2-63, 2-64).

Fig. 2-61

Fig. 2-62

Fig. 2-63

Fig. 2-64

三、左右开步

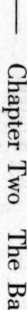

动作一:身体立正站立。右手叉腰,左手向左侧展开,掌心向左;松肩沉肘,目视前方(图 2-59)。

动作二:接上势,身体微右转,重心移至右腿,提左腿向左侧开步;同时左手顺缠走下弧里合,目视左前方(图 2-60)。

动作三:接上势,身体微左转,重心移至左腿,提右腿收于左腿内侧成并步;同时左手里合向上外翻逆缠向左开,目视左前方(图 2-61)。

此势主要是练习手合腿开、手开脚合及上引下进的方法,可根据场地反复练习。练毕左开步,练右开步,动作要领相同(图 2-62、2-63、2-64)。

4. Wave the hands with feet together

(1) Stand upright with feet together. Hang both hands naturally downward at the sides of body, the entire body relaxed. Eyes look ahead. Relax the right hip, turn the body slightly to the rightward, shift the weight to the right leg, lift the left leg and take a step leftward with the heel of left foot landing on the floor, the toes of foot hook upward. At the same time, move the right palm leftward and upward with the arm twining smoothly and then ward off it upward and leftward with the arm twining adversely. Close the left palm inward to in front of the abdomen. Eyes look to the forward-left (Fig.

2-65).

Fig. 2-65

Fig. 2-66

(2) Continuing from the previous movement. Turn the body slightly to the left, shift the weight to the left leg. Withdraw the right foot to the inside of the left foot. At the same time, ward off the left palm upward and leftward in an arc with the arm twining adversely. Close the right palm downward and leftward in an arc to in the front of abdomen. Eyes look to forward-right (Fig. 2-66). Repeat the previous exercise. And then take a step rightward, the essential points are the same as described in the previous exercise, reversing left and right. The footwork should be light and natural.

四、并步云手

动作一:立正,两手自然下垂于体侧,全身放松,眼平视前方。松右胯,身体微右转,重心移至右腿,提左腿向左开步,脚跟着地,脚尖上翘;同时右手先顺后逆缠走右上弧外扔,左手顺缠里合于腹前,目视左前方(图 2-65)。

动作二:接上势,身体微左转,重心移至左腿,右脚并步于左脚内侧;同时左手逆缠划弧外翻上掤,右手变顺缠走下弧合于腹前,眼看右前方(图 2-66)。如此开一步并一步,配合双手顺逆缠丝,练习周身上下相随的能力。步法要求轻灵自然,左右方向反复练习。

5. Wave hands in back cross-step

(1) Stand upright with feet together. Hang both hands naturally downward at the sides of body, the entire body relaxed. Eyes look ahead. Relax the right hip, turn the body slightly to the rightward, shift the weight to the right leg, lift the left leg and take a step leftward with the heel of left foot landing on the floor, the toes of foot hook upward. At the same time, move the right palm leftward and upward with the arm twining smoothly and then ward off it upward and leftward with the arm twining adversely. Close the left palm inward to in front of the abdomen. Eyes look to the forward-left (Fig. 2-67).

(2) Continuing from the previous movement. Move the right palm downward and leftward in an arc to the front of abdomen with the arm twining smoothly, the center of palm facing leftward. Ward off the left palm upward and leftward to the front of the left shoulder

with twining adversely, the center of the palm facing outward. At the same time, take a step to the rear-left of left foot with the right foot. Eyes look to forward-right (Fig. 2-68).

Fig. 2-67

Fig. 2-68

(3) Turn the body slightly to the right, the right palm moves leftward and upward with smooth twining and then ward off it leftward with reverse twining. Move the left palm downward and rightward in an arc to in the front of abdomen with the arm twining smoothly. At the same time, shift the weight to the right leg, lift the left leg and take a step leftward with the heel of left foot landing on the floor, the toes of the left foot hook upward. Eyes look to the forward-left of the body. Return the movement to the position as shown in Fig. 2-67. Repeat the previous exercise. And then take a step leftward, the essential points are the same as described in the previous exercise, reversing left and right.

五、插步云手

动作一:立正,两手自然下垂于体侧,全身放松,眼平视前方。松右胯,身体右转,重心移至右腿,提左腿向左开步,脚跟着地,脚尖上翘;同时右手先顺后逆缠丝走右上弧外掤,左手顺缠里合于腹前,目视左前方(图 2-67)。

动作二:接上势,右手顺缠里合于腹前,掌心朝左,左手逆缠外掤于左肩前,掌心朝外,同时右脚向左脚后插步,目视右前方(图 2-68)。

动作三:身体微右转,右手由顺缠变逆缠外翻上掤;左手顺缠走下弧,里合于腹前;同时重心移至右腿,提左腿向左开步,脚跟着地,脚尖上翘,目视身体左前方,恢复到如图 2-67 所示姿势。如此开一步,插一步,反复练习。

Chapter Three The Taiji Skills of Preserving Energy

第三章 太极培元养气法

The Taiji skills of preserving energy contain Sitting-quietly method, Stake exercises, lying exercise (not introduced temporarily). No matter what methods, all use the method of loosening the limbs, focusing mind and fixing intention to dig potentials of human bodies, decrease the metabolism, conciliate the seven emotions, making blood and energy mild, the channels smooth, so as to reach the aims of preserving health and benefiting wisdom and prolonging life.

太极培元养气法包括静坐养气法、桩功聚气法及卧功(卧功暂不介绍)。无论哪种方法,都是通过放松肢体、凝神固志等方法,来挖掘人体潜能,降低基础代谢,调和七情,使气血和顺,经络畅通,达到修养身心、益智延年的目的。

Section I Sitting-Quietly Method
第一节 静坐养气法

1. Preparation before sitting

You should loosen your clothes before beginning, then take some movements for a while to make the joints of muscle tendons stretched, so the vigor and blood get smooth. When you are sitting quietly, your back should not lean on the wall or other things, and you should pay attention to making air well through, avoiding being blew by wind and interrupted by others.

一、静坐前的准备

入坐前先宽松衣带,再活动关节片刻,使肌肉筋膜关节得以舒展,便于气血畅通。静坐时,背部不能靠墙或倚靠在其他物件上,同时要注意使空气流通,避免风吹,避免别人骚扰。

2. The posture of sitting-quietly

(1) Sitting freely

Sit on a wide stool or a board bed, with the two calves crossing freely, the two knees detached from the sitting surface. Face the south against the north. The two arms should be easy, forming arc. The palms should cross before abdomens, with the right palm on top, the left palm underneath, the palm cores all upward (Fig. 3-1).

Fig. 3-1

(2) Sitting flatly

The buttocks should sit on a wide stool or a board bed, with the two feet palms stepping on flatly on land, as wide as shoulders. The thighs should be right-angled with the calves, the two hand palms placing flat on the thighs, the palm cores upward or downward. The eyes can close slightly, or not at all. The posture when sitting quietly should be that the head must be upright and natural, the neck should be loosened, and can't be stiff. The body should be upright and steady, without bowing forward or facing upward, without leaning east or west. The chins should be controlled inward, with the lips and teeth closed slightly, the tip of toughs reaching the up cliffs of mouth, the eyes closed slightly, the face loosened naturally. The shoulders, arms, elbows, wrists all need to be loosened. The chest should be cherished, with the back stretched and loosened, the abdomen easy and quiet, the Huiyin lifted slightly.

Fig. 3-2

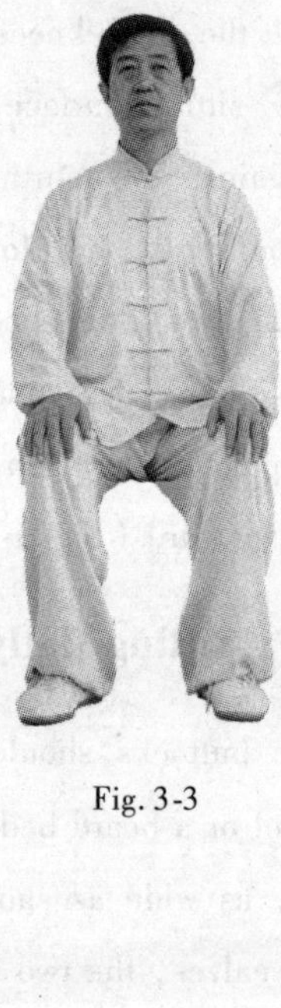

Fig. 3-3

二、静坐的姿势

(一)自由盘坐

坐于宽凳或硬板床上,两小腿自由交叉,两膝离开坐面。面南背北,两手臂放松,成圆弧形,手掌相叠于腹前,右掌在上,左掌在下,掌心均朝上(图 3-1)。

（二）平坐

臀部平坐于宽凳或木板床上，两脚掌平踏地，约与肩同宽。大腿与小腿约成直角，两手掌平放于大腿上，掌心朝上、朝下均可。眼可微闭，也可不闭。静坐时姿势要求头自然端正，颈部放松，不可僵硬。躯干正直稳固，不可前俯后仰，东倒西歪。下颏微向内收，唇齿微合，舌尖轻抵上腭，眼微闭，面容轻松自然。肩、臂、肘、腕皆要放松，胸微合，背舒展放松，腹部宽松镇定，会阴穴微微上提（图3-2、3-3）。

3. The key points of exercising

(1) Breathing naturally, guarding wills slightly

When the regulation of wills and breathing posture is finished, you may breath naturally, evenly and gently with the slight heaving of abdomen. When first exercises, to accumulate the vigor quickly, you may use the declining method to induce. It is to say, inhaling naturally without the will, the two ears should hear quietly the exhaling of yourself, do not emit coarse sound. With exhaling the wills are loosened from heart to lower abdomen to make the heart energy decline into the Dantian. Persistent exercising will make Dantian give off heat. When the Dantian gives off heat rather distinctly, stop inducing and declining the vigor, let the weak wills, continuous breath end at the Dantian, preserving the energy.

When exercising, you must concentrate your wills on the Dantian (meaning lower abdomen universally). Your wills must be light. You should not guard them nervously. The more peaceful and more weak your wills are, the more easily the energy assembles at the Dantian and goes through the channels. Nevertheless nervous thoughts and anxiously seeking success may influence the normal running of the energy. "Being weak and windy, the energy will follow you." in《the Sutra of inside》is meant this. The more relaxed your body is and the more peaceful your thoughts are, the more vigorous your energy is, the more smoothly it runs.

(2) Insisting in it and gradually progressing

When exercising sitting quietly first, just breath naturally. With going deep into the exercise, you can process to even, gentle, deep and slow abdomen internal breath. The abdomen internal breath is formed through persistent exercising according to the normal exercising method, but is not done easily by beginners. So the beginners may not take back the breath deliberately and make long the breath against natural rules to reach deep, long, even and thin breath. Breathing 12-14 times per minute for beginners and 2-3 times per minute for masters can satisfy the need usually.

(3) Obviating useless ideas and eliminating tension

The appearance of useless ideas is a necessary phenomenon while beginning, and will infect the effect. But you must not be tense for it, because useless ideas can be obviated. With mastering of the exercises, useless ideas could be decreased gradually, at last disappear. Some simple and effective methods are introduced below:

① Counting breath

Counting your breath silently when exercising. One exhaling and inhaling is called one time. This is the method of replacing millions of ideas with one idea.

② Method of persuading

When the useless ideas such as trivia appear during exercising, persuade yourself that you should exercise attentively, the other things could be done after the exercising, it is useless to think about it now. Exercise it securely. Persuade yourself for some times, then the useless ideas will decrease gradually.

③ Killing the heart ghost with Sharp sword

During exercising when your useless ideas are too heavy to be eliminated, or false vision appears making you addicted to it hard to be pulled out, open your eyes immediately, and all the ideas and false vision will disappear soon. Because the ghost is induced from heart, so it names "Killing heart ghost with sharp sword". You can exercise in succession after those ideas disappear.

(4) Take it naturally and guard Dantian tightly

After some time of sitting quietly and exercising, the inside or surface of body will have this or that kind of feelings, such as cold, warm, light, heavy, deep, cool, tingle, bulge, itch etc. At first, the tips of limbs feel most distinctly, then there are intestinal sounds, successively there appear cool, warm, muscle bouncing, tingle and bulge etc. It varies with different constitutions of each body. This feeling is normal reactions of exercising, named "accepting the energy". Sometimes there will appear visions such as hills, water and human. You may not be nervous and afraid, and may not seek them to avoid "enthrallment". These things are false, and are wry reflections of the external world in brains. You should neglect the hallucinations, guard Dantian gently, the hallucinations will disappear naturally. Not be surprised on seeing surprise, the surprise will not be surprise. Varieties of visions will calm down with mastering of the exercise, and renew to a quiet, windy, peaceful state. At this time, the heart is as quiet as still water, useless ideas do not rise, the breath is continuous and the wills are like or not like in existence. Then you will taste the weak and windy ambit, and your breathing method will get into the inside breath of abdomen naturally.

三、练功要领

(一)自然呼吸,轻守意念

意念与呼吸姿势调整好后,随着腹部轻微的一起一伏,伴以均匀、柔和的自然呼吸。初练时,为了快速聚气,可采用下沉法引导,即自然吸气,不加意念;两耳静听自己呼气,不使之发出粗糙的声音,随呼气意念从心窝松到小腹,使心气下沉于丹田。如此持久练习,丹田会渐渐发热,待丹田发热较明显时,停止引气下沉,使恬淡的意念,绵绵的呼吸轻轻止于丹田,养气。

练功时,思想集中在丹田(泛指小腹),意念要轻,不可紧张死守,意识越清静、越恬淡,体内真气越容易在丹田汇聚和在经络中流通。而思想紧张,急于求成,反而影响真气的正常运行。《内经》:“恬淡虚无,真气从之”即是此意。身体越放松,思想越清静,内气就越旺盛,内气运行也越顺畅。

(二)持之心恒,循序渐进

初练静坐,自然呼吸即可。随着练功的深入,逐渐过渡到均匀、柔和、深长缓慢的腹式内呼吸。腹式内呼吸是按照正确的练功方法,通过持之心恒的练功后自然形成的,并非初学者可以一下子做到的。因此初学者不可为了使呼吸达到深长匀细而故意憋气,拉长呼吸,失去自然规律。初练者一般每分钟呼吸 12 ~ 14 次,功深者每分钟呼吸 2 ~ 3 次即足以保证需要。

(三)排除杂念,消除紧张

杂念的出现是练功初期的必然现象,会影响功效。但不必因此紧张,因为杂念是可以排除的。随着功夫的加深,杂念会渐渐减少,直至消失。

下面介绍几种简单有效的方法:

1. 数息法

练功时默数自己呼吸次数,一呼一吸为一次,从 1 往后数。这是以一念代万念之法。

2. 规劝法

练功中出现生活琐事等杂念时,劝告自己:“现在应专心练功,其他事待练功结束再做,现在多想也没用,安心练功吧。”如此劝告自己几遍，杂念会渐渐减少。

3. 慧剑斩心魔

闭目练功时，杂念过重，难以消除，或出现幻景，沉湎其中难以自拔时，立即睁开双眼，这时一切杂念及幻景立即消失。因魔由心起，故名之"慧剑斩心魔"。待杂念消失后再继续练功。

（四）听其自然，守住丹田

经过一段时间静坐练功，机体内部或体表将产生这样或那样的感觉，如冷、暖、轻、重、沉、凉、麻、胀、痒等现象。起初，一般以四肢末梢感觉最明显，渐有肠鸣咕咕之声，进而全身或局部清凉、温暖、肌肉跳动、麻胀等现象，因个人体质不同而各异。这些感觉是练功的正常反应，称之为"得气"。有时还会出现山、水、人物等幻景，都不必紧张害怕，更不能追求，以免"着相"。这些东西都是虚幻不实的，是大脑对客观世界的歪曲反映。对所有的幻觉都不动心，不予理睬，只管轻轻守住丹田，幻景自会消失。见怪不怪，其怪自败。各种动象都将随着功夫的加深逐渐平静下来，恢复到安静、虚无、平和的状态。这时心如止水，杂念不起，呼吸绵绵，意念似有似无，若隐若现，真正体会到恬淡虚无的境界，呼吸方式也就自然过渡到腹式内呼吸了。

4. Drawing in exercises

The two hands should cover on Dantian and knead clockwise for 36 circles with Dantian as the core, and gradually widen the area to the chest and abdomen; then knead anticlockwise for 24 circles, and lessen the circle to end at Dantian. After this, knead hot your hand palms, wipe your face 12 times (strengthening the spleens), knead hot your thumb backs and wipe your eyepits 12 times (lighting your eyes). The two hand palms press your ears forward, touch on the ear holes. Beat the Fengfu 36 times with forefingers and middle fingers, then knead the legs and feet for a while. Stand up slowly, to end the exercise.

Attention:

You should exercise hard with a balky, serious, cautious and honest spirit, but should not emphasize the result. The elder said: "You may not guard with mind, may not seek without mind. Use mind will be enthralled, not use mind will fail. It is better to seem to guard or seem not to, be lingering and seem to exist." The general principle is: Seek reassurance, be solid in heart. Don't forget, don't help, exercise intentionally, and succeed inadvertently.

四、收功

两手覆于丹田上，以丹田为中心，顺时针揉36圈，面积扩大到胸腹；再反方向揉24圈，圈渐渐缩小，止于丹田。揉毕搓热双掌，擦脸12次（健脾），双手大拇背搓热，擦眼眶12次（明目），两手掌将耳翼向前压，紧贴耳孔，以食、中二指敲击风府穴36次，然后按摩双腿、双脚片刻，慢慢起身，练功结束。

注意：

要本着执著、严肃、谨慎、真诚的练功精神刻苦练功，但不可执著功效。古人云:“不可用心守,不可无意求,用心着相,无意落空,似守非守,绵绵若存。”总体原则是:求放心,不动心,勿忘勿助,有意练功,无意成功。

SectionII Stake Exercise

第二节 桩功聚气法

1. The method of taking energy

1) Stand upright with feet shoulder-with apart, keep the body upright and relaxed, the knees bent and hips relaxed. Hang arms naturally down at sides of thighs. Keep the head upright, eyes closed slightly, look Dantian in mind. With the lips and teeth closed slightly, the tip of tongue touching the upper palate of mouth, breathing naturally (Fig. 3-4)

2) Continue from previous movement. Raise the both palms naturally upward in respective sides of body to the head level with the arms turning outward and smoothly twining. Inhale in the movement (Fig. 3-5).

3) Without stopping previous movement. Move the both palms upward and close them to above the forehead with the centers of palms facing downward, the arms with adverse twining, finish the inhaling (Fig. 3-6).

Fig. 3-4

Fig. 3-5

Fig. 3-6

Fig. 3-7

Fig. 3-8

4) To exhale, following the lowering of the body, move the both palms downward past the front of chest, the energy flows to Dantian (Fig. 3-7). And then continue relax and lower the body to make the energy flows to soles, finish the exhaling (Fig. 3-8).

5) Return to starting position. Inhale when raising palms and exhaling when lowering the palms. Repeat these movements many times, to make the energy flowing the upper and lower parts of body.

Key to the movement: When practising, the breathing should be even, gentle and deep, it following the movement, it is not done easily by beginners. So the beginners may not do it. When inhaling, collect the soul of heaven and earth, from the Baihui nourish body and eliminate the gas of disease and dirty from Yongquan to improve health.

一、采气法

动作一:两脚开立,与肩同宽。屈膝松胯,立身中正,全身放松,两臂自然下垂于体侧;头自然正,二目微闭,内视丹田,唇齿微合,舌尖轻抵上腭,自然呼吸(图3-4)。

动作二:接上势,两臂慢慢自然顺缠外翻向左右两侧上升与头顶相平,吸气(图3-5)。

动作三:上动不停,两手继续上升逆缠里合于头上额前,掌心朝下,吸气尽(图3-6)。

动作四:呼气,两掌随身体下沉经胸前下沉,经丹田时稍停

（图 3-7），然后继续放松下沉，意念气沉脚底，呼气尽（图 3-8）。

动作五：还原，再上升吸气，下沉呼气，反复练习，使身体内部有上下贯通之气感。

要求：在练习时，呼吸要深长、匀细。初学者不易做到，不必强为，随呼吸自然动作。吸气时采天地清灵之气，由百会贯于丹田，充实全身，行于涌泉，循环不已，体内浊气、病气自然排出体外。

2. The method of grasping the energy

1) Stand at attention, keep the head upright and naturally, the neck relaxed, the lips and teeth closed slightly, the tip of tongue reaching the upper jaw. Breathe naturally. Eyes look ahead (Fig. 3-9).

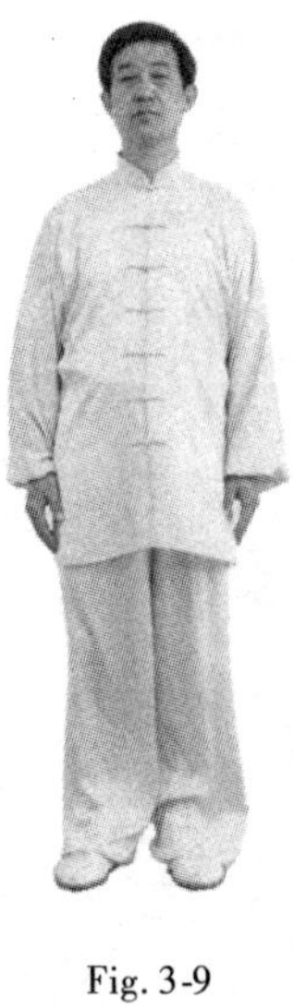
Fig. 3-9

Fig. 3-10

Fig. 3-11

2) Continue from previous movement. Take a step forward with the left foot to form a left bow step and push palms upward and forward in arcs. Exhale in the movement. Eyes look forward (Fig. 3-10).

3) Without stopping previous movement. Shift the center of gravity downward and backward in and arc, clench the palms into fists and grasp the energy downward to Dantian, inhale in the movements. Eyes look forward (Fig. 3-11, 3-12).

4) Continue from previous movement. Change the both fists into palms and push both palms upward from Dantian to the front, exhale in the movement (Fig. 3-13).

Key to the movement: Repeat these movements in the right and left sides, so the emptiness and solid change smoothly, the Dantian and the Mingmen may concentrate on each other.

Fig. 3-12

Fig. 3-13

二、抓气法

动作一:立正。屈膝松胯,含胸塌腰,头自然正,颈部放松,唇齿微合,舌尖轻抵上腭,眼平视前方(图3-9)。自然呼吸。

动作二:接上势,左脚向前开步成左弓步,两手走上弧向前推出,目视前方,呼气(图3-10)。

动作三:上动不停,重心走弧线后移,两掌变拳抓气下沉,收于丹田,目视前方(图3-11、3-12)。此动吸气。

动作四:接上势,随呼气双拳变掌由丹田走上弧前推(图3-13)。

要求:上述动作反复练习,左右均可,使虚实转换圆转自如,丹田与命门相吸相通。

3. The Method of transporting Dantian

1) Stand upright with feet are shoulder-width apart, the knees bent and hips relaxed. Eyes closed slightly, the tip of tongue touching the upper plate, breathing naturally. Place the left palm on the navel, the right palm pressing on the back of left palm (Fig. 3-14).

2) Follow the turning of body and changing of the emptiness and solidness, both hands rub around clockwise for 36 circles with the navel as cover, and gradually wider the area to the chest and abdomen, coordinate with the counterclockwise 24 circles, withdraw them on the navel (Fig. 3-15, 3-16).

Fig. 3-14

Fig. 3-15

Fig. 3-16

Attention: The women may rub both hands around in counter-clockwise for 36 circles first, and then rub both hands around in clockwise 24 circles, the places of the hands are opposite with the man.

三、丹田内转运气法

动作一:两脚开立,比肩略宽,屈膝松胯,二目微闭内视,唇齿微合,舌尖轻抵上腭,呼吸自然,左手心覆盖于脐上,右手掌盖在左手背上(图3-14)。

动作二:结合身法,虚实转换,两手顺时针以肚脐为中心,由小到大转36圈,直到上胸下腹,配合自然呼吸;再换右手在下,左手在上逆时针方向,由大到小转24圈收于肚脐(图

3-15、3-16）。

注意：女士先逆转 36 圈，再顺转 24 圈，双手上下位置与男子相反。

4. Hunyuan stake

Fig. 3-17

The side of fig. 3-17

Stand upright with feet parting wider than the shoulder, keep the entire body upright and relaxed, the knees bent and hips relaxed, the head and neck upright and relaxed. The mouth and teeth closed slightly, the tip of tongue touching the upper plate. Put the both palms in the front of chest with arms in a circular form, the centers of palms facing inward and the fingers pointing each other, the shoulders relaxed and elbows lowered. The crotch should be round, the feet stand firmly, the toes, outsides of the soles and heels grasping on the floor, the Yongquan should be empty, keep the body weight between the both legs (Fig. 3-17, the side of Fig. 3-17).

Key to the movement: Concentrate on the movement, relax the all parts of body.

四、浑元桩

两脚开立,比肩略宽,屈膝松胯,含胸塌腰,立身中正,全身放松。头正,微上顶,颈部放松,唇齿微合,舌尖轻抵上腭。两臂弧形环抱于胸前,手心朝里,指尖相对,肩松肘沉。裆要开圆,脚踏实地,脚趾、脚外侧、脚跟皆抓地,涌泉穴要虚,重心在两腿之间(图 3-17、3-17 附图)。

要求:思想清静而集中,全身放松,任大气自然流行。

5. Drawing in exercises

The methods of drawing in exercises are same as in the Sitting-quietly exercises.

五、收功

收功方法与静坐养气法收功相同,不再述。

Chapter Four The Cream Eighteen Forms of Chen-Style Taijiquan

第四章 陈氏太极拳精要十八式

Section I Names of Movements in the Cream Eighteen Forms of Chen-Style Taijiquan

第一节 动作名称

Form 1 Starting Form

Form 2 Buddha's Warrior Attendant Pounds Mortar

Form 3 Lazy About Trying Robe

Form 4 Six Sealings and Four Closings

Form 5 Single Whip

Form 6 White Crane Spreads Its Wings

Form 7 Walk Obliquely

Form 8 Brush Knee

Form 9 Twist Step

Form 10 Cover Hands and Strike with Arm

Form 11 Pat High on the Horse

Form 12　Kick with the Left Heel

Form 13　Jade Girl Works at Shuttles

Form 14　Wave Hands Like Cannon

Form 15　Turn Body with Lotus Kick

Form 16　Strike Face Like Cannon

Form 17　Buddha ' s Warrior Attendant Pounds Mortar

Form 18　Finishing Form

第一式　太极起势

第二式　金刚捣碓

第三式　懒扎衣

第四式　六封四闭

第五式　单鞭

第六式　白鹅亮翅

第七式　斜行

第八式　搂膝

第九式　拗步

第十式　掩手肱拳

第十一式　高探马

第十二式　左蹬一根

第十三式　玉女穿梭

第十四式　云手

第十五式　转身双摆莲

第十六式　当头炮

第十七式　金刚捣碓

第十八式　收势

Section II Diagrams of The Cream Eighteen Forms of Chen Style Taijiquan
第二节 动作图解

Form 1 Staring Form

1. Stand naturally upright with feet together at attention. Put the hands naturally down by the sides of the body, palms inward and lightly against the outer sides of the thighs. Keep the head upright naturally, and close the mouth lightly, with the tongue at the upper jaw. Eyes look straight ahead (Fig. 4-1).

Fig. 4-1

2. Continuing from previous movement. Slowly bend the both knees and relax the hips, take a step leftward with the left foot, so the feet parting a little wider than shoulder, toes pointing slightly outward. The chest held slightly inward, back extended and the shoulders relaxed, the elbows lowered. Keep the head and the body upright and natural, the top of the head is raised lightly in the mind. Eyes look straight ahead (Fig. 4-2).

Key to the movement: Taking the step with the left foot, the center of gravity moving onto the right foot, then lift the left foot, land the toes first on the floor, followed gradually by the entire sole. The entire body is relaxed naturally, the vigor flowing to the Dantian. Bending the knees and relaxing the hips, use the nose to exhale deeply.

3. Continuing from previous movement. Raise the both arms slowly upward and forward to shoulder level, palms facing downward. At the same time, bend knees and relax hips, the body lowering downward slightly. Eyes look forward (Fig. 4-3).

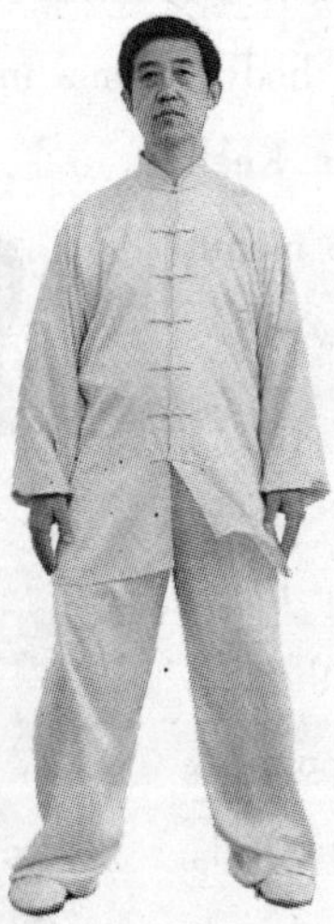

Fig. 4-2

Fig. 4-3

Key to the movement: In raising the both arms and lowering the body, the muscles of the chest, back, ribs and abdomen must be relaxed, and avoid shrugging the shoulders, using the nose to inhale.

4. Continuing from previous movement. As the weight descend, the knees bending and hips relaxing, press the both palms downward to the front of abdomen, the palms facing downward (Fig. 4-4).

Key to the movement: In pressing palms downward, keep the upper body erect, back extend, buttocks held slightly in and the groin is opened slightly. Using the nose to exhale.

Fig. 4-4

第一式 太极起势

动作一:两脚并立,成立正姿势。两臂下垂于身体两侧,手心向内,头自然正,唇齿微合,舌尖轻抵上腭,二目平视(图 4-1)。

动作二:接上势,屈膝松胯,放松下沉,提左脚向左横开一步,比两肩略宽,脚尖微外摆,脚趾、脚掌外缘、脚后跟皆要抓地,涌泉穴要虚,含胸塌腰,松肩沉肘,立身中正,头自然正直,虚领顶劲,二目平视(图 4-2)。

要求:横开步时,重心先移到右腿,提左脚开步,脚尖先着地,慢慢踏平。周身放松,气沉丹田,降于涌泉,屈膝松胯,下沉时呼气。

此时脑空心静,思想高度集中,心中无一所念,浑然如一片无极景象。

动作三:接上势,两手缓缓上升与肩平,手心向下,松肩沉肘;随两手上升,身体慢慢下降,屈膝松胯,两脚踏实,二目平视(图4-3)。

要求:当两手上升、身体下降时,胸、背、肋、腹各部肌肉均要松弛下沉,促使心气下降,切忌肩上耸,横气填胸。此动吸气。

动作四:接上势,身体继续下沉,屈膝松胯,两手随身体下按至腹前,手心向下,二目平视(图4-4)。

要求:两手下按时,要立身中正,切忌弯腰突臀,裆部要松、虚、活。下蹲时,如坐凳子一样。此动呼气。

Form 2　Buddha's Warrior Attendant Pounds Mortar

1. Continuing from previous movement. Turn the upper body slightly leftward and shift the weight to the right. Move the both palms upward to the forward-left of the body in arcs, the left arm twining adversely and the right arm twining smoothly, ward off the left palm to the upper side of the left knee with the palm facing outward, at the eyes level. Ward off the right palm to the middle line of the front of body with the palm facing upward. Eyes look forward-left (Fig. 4-5).

Key to the movement: Turning the body and relaxing the hips must be coordinated. As rotating arms inward or outward, the arms should possess a certain twining power.

Fig. 4-5

Fig. 4-6

2. Continuing from previous movement. Turn the upper body rightward about 90 degrees, the toes of the right foot turning outward and the center of gravity shifting onto the left leg. At the same time, deflect the both palms rightward in arcs with left arm twining smoothly and right arm twining adversely. Using the nose to exhale in the movement. Eyes look forward-left (Fig. 4-6).

Fig. 4-7

3. Continuing from previous movement. Shift the center of gravity onto the right leg and lift the left leg with knee bent. Bend the right knee slightly and relax the right hip, lower the upper body and turn it slightly to the right, ward off the both palms upward and rightward in arcs. Eyes look forward-left (Fig. 4-7).

Key to the movement: Lowering the body and lifting the left leg must be coordinated, don't bend the upper body forward and protrude the buttocks out. In the movement use the nose to inhale.

4. Continuing from previous movement. Move the left foot a step to the forward-left sliding the inside of the heel along the floor, the toes of the left foot hooked and turned inward. At the same time, continue warding off the both palms to the rear-right, the palms facing outward. Eyes look forward-left (Fig. 4-8).

Fig. 4-8

Fig. 4-9

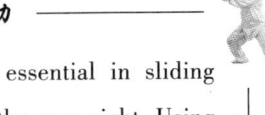

Key to the movement: Coordination is essential in sliding with left heel while warding off both palms to the rear-right. Using the nose to inhale in the movement.

5. Continuing from previous movement. Move the center of gravity to the left leg as the sole of the left foot is placed on floor. With the moving of weight, turn the upper body leftward 45degrees, move both palms downward and forward in an arcs with the left arm twining adversely and the right arm twining smoothly, the left palm moves to in the front of the left side of chest, elbow bent, palm facing downward. The right palm moves to beside the right knee, palm facing obliquely downward, the fingers pointing backward. Eyes look forward (Fig. 4-9).

Key to the movement: Turning the body, shifting the weight and moving the both palms must be coordinated. In the movement use the nose to inhale then exhale.

6. Continuing from previous movement. Move the center of gravity onto the left leg, turn the body to the left and step with the right foot to in the front of the left foot only the toes touching the floor to form a right empty step. At the same time, the right palm performs an uppercut in an upward and forward arc to in the front of the right side of the chest. The left palm moves forward, upward in a curve and is then placed on the right forearm, palm facing downward. Eyes look forward (Fig. 4-10).

Key to the movement: Stepping with the right foot, the knees bent and hips relaxed, the footwork light. Using the nose to inhale in the movement.

Fig. 4-10

Fig. 4-11

7. Continuing from previous movement: The left palm twines smoothly from inside to outside and lower it to in the front of abdomen, the palm facing upward. At the same time, clench the fingers of the right hand into a fist and fall it into the center of the left palm. Eyes look forward (Fig. 4-11).

Key to the movement: The distance about 8-10cm between the arms and the body, the arms collecting the proper warding off power. Lowering the left fist, the waist relaxed. Using the nose to exhale.

8. Continuing from previous movement. The right fist twines adversely and raises it up to the shoulder level in the front of body. At the same time, lift the right leg with the knee bent and hips relaxed,

the toes pointing naturally downward. Eyes look forward (Fig. 4-12).

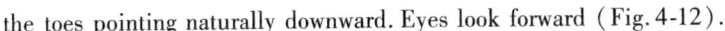

Key to the movement: Lowering the body and lifting the right leg must be coordinated. Raising the right fist, the shoulder relaxed and elbow lowered, standing on the left leg steady. Using the nose to inhale.

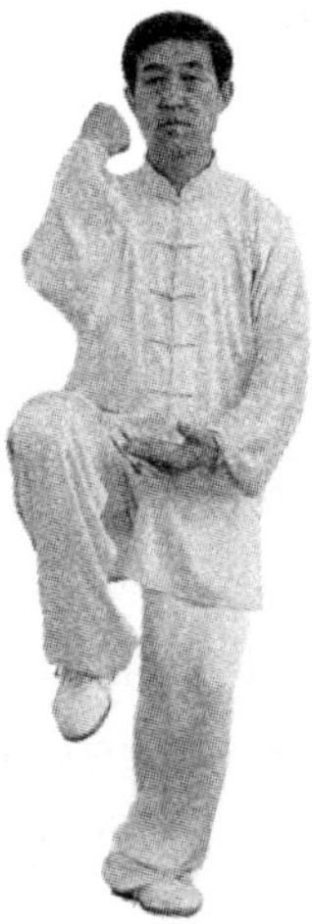

Fig. 4-12

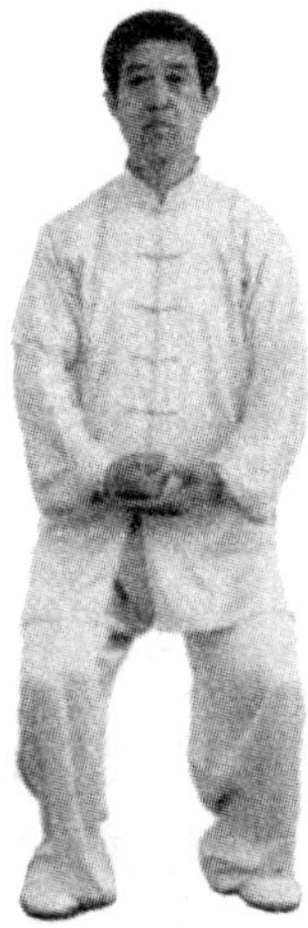

Fig. 4-13

9. Continuing from previous movement. Stamp the right foot on the floor about shoulder—width apart to the inside of the left foot, the sloe of the right foot is placed on the floor. At the same time, smash the right fist downward onto the center of the left palm, the arms bent. Eyes look forward (Fig. 4-13).

Key to the movement: Stamping the right foot and smashing the right fist be completed in a coordinated movement. As stamping the right foot, knees bent, hips relaxed, entire sole flat on the floor. Using the nose to exhale, the vigor settling Dantian.

第二式 金刚捣碓

动作一:接上势,身体微向左转,重心右移,两手左逆缠右顺缠,走弧线向左前上方掤出,左手掤至左膝上方与眼平,手心朝外,右手掤至胸前中线,手心朝上,目视左前方(图 4-5)。

要求:上掤转体时,要结合裆腰劲,松胯塌腰,劲贯手掌。此动吸气。

动作二:接上势,身体右转 90 度,重心由右移到左腿,右脚尖外摆,两手左顺右逆缠向右后攌,目视左前方(图 4-6)。此动呼气。

动作三:接上势,重心移至右腿,左腿提起,里合扣裆,屈膝松胯,身体下沉且微向右转,两手上掤,目视左前方(图 4-7)。

要求:左腿上提,身体下沉,上下相合。切忌弯腰突臀。此动吸气。

动作四:接上势,左脚跟内侧着地,向左前方铲地滑出,脚尖上翘里合,重心在右腿;两手继续向右后上方加掤劲,目视左前方(图 4-8)。

要求:向前开步时,身法要端正,左脚向左前开步,两手向右上掤,形成对称。此动呼气。

动作五:接上势,重心由右腿移到左腿,左脚尖外摆踏平。身体随重心移动,向左转 45 度,两手左逆右顺缠,走下弧向前掤,左手掤至胸前,手心朝下;右手下沉至右膝内上方,手心朝外,指尖朝后,目视前方(图 4-9)。

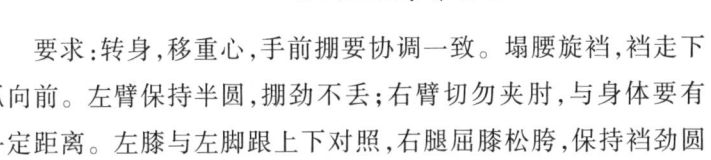

要求:转身,移重心,手前掤要协调一致。塌腰旋裆,裆走下弧向前。左臂保持半圆,掤劲不丢;右臂切勿夹肘,与身体要有一定距离。左膝与左脚跟上下对照,右腿屈膝松胯,保持裆劲圆活。此动先吸气后呼气。

动作六:接上势,左手向前撩掌,向上再向内环绕合于胸前右小臂内侧;右手领右脚弧线向前上托掌于右胸前与左手相合,左手心朝下。右脚经左脚内侧向前上步,脚尖点地,重心在左腿,目视前方(图 4-10)。

要求:上步时,要屈膝松胯,轻灵自然,稳重,两手与身体有上下相合之意。此动吸气。

动作七:接上势,左手顺缠外翻下沉于腹前,手心朝上;右手握拳下沉落于左掌心内,拳心朝上,目视前方(图 4-11)。

要求:两手与身体间距 8 ~ 10 厘米,有圆掤之感;随落拳腰劲下沉。此动呼气。

动作八:接上势,右拳逆缠向上提起,与右肩平,左腿屈膝松胯,提起右腿旋于裆内,脚尖自然下垂,目视前方(图 4-12)。

要求:提腿时,身体要下沉,有上下相合之意;提拳时要松肩沉肘,促使内气下降,支撑要稳。此动吸气。

动作九:接上势,右脚震脚落地,脚掌踏平,两脚间距约与肩同宽;右拳顺缠下落于左掌心,两臂撑圆,目视前方(图 4-13)。

要求:右拳、右脚同时下沉,震脚发劲,屈膝松胯,气沉丹田。此动呼气。

Form 3 Lazy About Trying Robe

1. Turn the body slightly to the left and move the center of gravity rightward. Change the right fist into a palm and move it leftward, upward and rightward in an arc to in the forward-right of the head with the right arm twining adversely, press the left palm to beside the left hip with the arm twining adversely. Eyes look forward-left (Fig. 4-14).

Fig. 4-14

Fig. 4-15

Key to the movement: In warding off the right palm and pressing the left palm, the application of opening power is required in it.

2. Continuing from previous movement. The right palm moves

rightward, downward and upward in an arc, the left palm moves leftward, upward and downward in an arc, cross the both forearms in the front of the chest, the right hand on outside, the right palm facing upward, the left palm facing outward. Shift the center of gravity onto the left leg, take a step rightward with the right foot, the inside of the right heel sliding the floor, the toes hooked and turned inward. Eyes look rightward (Fig. 4-15).

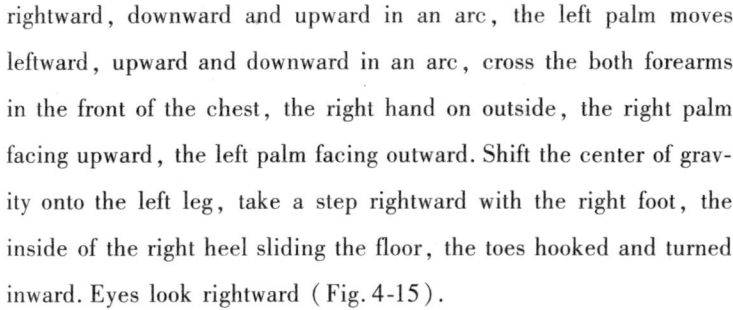

Key to the movement: Taking the step with the right foot must be coordinated with closing the both hands in the chest, the footwork light, using the nose to exhale.

3. Continuing form previous movement. Turn the upper body to the left, the center of gravity moving rightward. The right palm moves upward and rightward in an arc with right arm twining smoothly. Eyes look forward-right (Fig. 4-16).

Key to the movement: Moving the center of gravity, the both arms remaining the ward-off force, the groin relaxed and opened, use the nose to inhale in the movement.

4. Continuing from previous movement. Turn the upper body to the right, the center of gravity moving rightward. Move

Fig. 4-16

the right palm upward and rightward in an arc with the right arm twining adversely to the upside of the right knee, the fingers at eyes level. The left palm twines smoothly downward passing to abdomen to beside the left side of body, the part between thumb and index finger touching the left side of the waist, the center of hand facing downward. Eyes follow the right hand then look forward (Fig. 4-17).

Fig. 4-17

Key to the movement: Moving the right palm, the power flowing through waist, shoulder and arm and ultimately get to the fingertips. In the final position, the hips and waist relaxed, the groin opened, the shoulders and elbows lowered. The left knee bent slightly and toes of the left foot turned inward. The upper body erect, continue to exhale in the movement.

第三式 懒 扎 衣

动作一:身体微左转,重心右移。右拳变掌,逆缠上掤于头右侧,左手逆缠下按至左胯侧,目视左前方(图 4-14)。

要求:右拳变掌上掤时,先塌腰旋转,以身催手,弧线上掤,与左手下按配合,形成开劲。此动吸气。

动作二:接上势,两手由双逆缠变双顺缠划弧交叉于胸前,左手合于右臂内,手心朝外,右手心朝上;重心移至左腿,提右腿向横开一大步,脚跟内侧着地,脚尖上翘里合,目视身体右方(图 4-15)。

要求:手合脚开同时进行并协同一致,手到脚到,开步要轻灵自然。此动呼气。

动作三:接上势,身体左转,重心右移,右手顺缠上掤,目视右前方(图 4-16)。

要求:移重心时,裆走后圆弧,左肘掤劲不丢,右腋不能夹死,有圆虚之感。此动吸气。

动作四:接上势,身体向右转,右手逆缠外开至右膝上方,松肩沉肘,略变顺缠,指尖高与眼平;左手顺缠经腹前至身本左侧,变逆缠叉腰,四指在前,拇指在后。重心在右腿,眼随右手转视前方(图 4-17)。

要求:开右手时,以腰催肩,劲到松肩,以肩催肘,劲到沉肘,略坐腕,劲贯于指尖。松胯塌腰,开裆贵圆,右实左虚,右膝与脚跟上下对照,不能前倾、后倒、外撇;左腿挺而不直,膝微屈,脚尖内扣。立身中正,舒展大方。此势继续呼气。

Form 4 Six Sealings and Four Closing

1. Continuing form previous movement. Turn the upper body to the right and move the center of gravity slightly rightward. Extend the left palm to the inside of the right forearm and lower the right

palm slightly. Eyes look at the right palm (Fig. 4-18).

Fig. 4-18

Key to the movement: Closing the both palms, turning the body rightward and moving the weight rightward must be coordinated. The both wrists bent slightly up, use the nose to inhale.

2. Continuing from previous movement. Turn the upper body to the left and move the center of gravity leftward. At the same time, deflect the both palms downward and leftward in arcs with the left arm twining adversely and the right arm twining smoothly. Eyes look forward-right (Fig. 4-19).

Fig. 4-19

Key to the movement: Deflecting the both palms downward and leftward, the palms remaining the closing power and warding-off force. The waist relaxed and the weight lowered, use the nose to exhale.

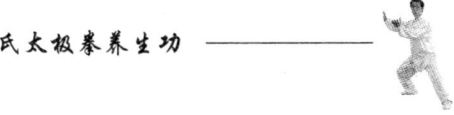

3. Continuing from previous movement. Continue to turn the body leftward and move the center of gravity to the right. Continue to move both palms leftward and backward in an arcs with the left arm twining adversely and the right arm twining smoothly. Eyes look forward-left (Fig. 4-20).

Fig. 4-20

Key to the movement: The arms remaining the ward-off fore, use the nose inhale in the movement.

4. Without stopping previous movement. Continue to turn the body to the right and move the center of gravity rightward. Move the both palms leftward, upward in arcs to the front of the left shoulder with left arm twining smoothly and the right arm twining adversely. Eyes look to forward-right (Fig. 4-21).

Key to movement: While changing from deflecting to raising the palms, the waist serves as an axis, the shoulders and elbows lowered, continue to inhale in the movement.

5. Continuing from previous movement. The upper body turn to the right, press both palms rightward and downward to in the front

of the right side of the abdomen. At the same time, shift the center of gravity onto the right leg and move the left foot to the inside of the right foot so that the feet about 20cm apart, the toes of the left foot on the floor. Eyes look the palms (Fig. 4-22).

Fig. 4-21

Fig. 4-22

Key to the movement: Pressing both palms downward, turning the body and moving the weight must be well coordinated, the waist extent, hips relaxed, the shoulders and elbows lowered, use the nose to exhale in the movement.

第四式　六封四闭

动作一：接上势，身体右转，重心略右移，左手从腰间走上弧与右手相合;右手略前引下沉,目视右手中指端(图 4-18)。

要求:左手与右手相合时,与身体右转、重心右移相结合,两手坐腕接劲。此动吸气。

动作二:接上势,身体左转,重心左移,两手左逆右顺缠,自右而向左攦,目视右前方(图 4-19)。

要求:下攦时,重心下沉,塌腰,两手合劲不丢,加外掤劲。此动呼气。

动作三:接上势,身体继续左转,两手继续左逆右顺缠,向左后上方攦,重心右移,目视左前方(图 4-20)。

要求:攦时,两手不能偏后,右臂掤劲不能丢。此动吸气。

动作四:上动不停,重心继续右移,两手变左顺右逆缠向上划弧,合于左肩时,身体略右转,目视右前方(图 4-21)。

要求:在由攦变按时,两手下攦上合,均由裆腰左移右旋,松肩沉肘,旋腕转膀,使劲不丢不顶,圆转自如,转折顺遂。此动继续吸气。

动作五:接上势,重心不变,身体微右转下沉,两手合力走弧线向右前下方按,左脚收于右脚内侧 20 厘米处,脚尖点地。目视右前下方(图 4-22)。

要求:双手下按时,要松胯塌腰,松肩沉肘,两手合力随身体下沉前要协调一致。此动呼气。

Form 5 Single Whip

1. Continuing from previous movement: Turn the upper body to the right slightly, move the left palm forward and the right palm

backward, the both arms twining smoothly so that the palms facing upward. With the turning of the body, the left knee turned inward, using the toes of the left foot as a pivot. Eyes look at the both palms (Fig. 4-23).

Key to the movement: The hands twining around in a small circle following the leftward and rightward turning of the body.

2. Continuing from previous movement. Turn the upper body to the left and turn the left knee outward using the toes of left foot as a pivot. Bunch the fingers of the right hand into a hook-hand and raise it to the upper-right, at the shoulder level, the tip of hook-hand pointing downward, Move the left palm backward to in the front of the abdomen, the elbow bent. Eyes look at the right hand (Fig. 4-24).

Fig. 4-23

Fig. 4-24

Fig. 4-25

Key to the movement: Raising the right hook-hand and turning of the body must be well coordinated, and using the waist as an axis to initiate the movements of the arms. Throughout the movement, the waist and shoulders are relaxed, elbows lowered. It is a closing movement, use the nose to exhale in the movement.

3. Continuing from previous movement. Turn the upper body to the right, shift the center of gravity onto the right leg and lift the left leg with the knee bent and turned inward. The back of the right hand as force point, the shoulders an elbows lowered. Eyes look forward-left (Fig. 4-25).

Key to the movement: Do not curve the torso and protrude the buttocks out. The posture is a closing movement, use the nose to inhale in it.

4. Continuing from previous movement. Shift the weight onto the right leg. Take a step to the left with the left foot, sliding the inside of the left heel along the floor, the toes hooked upward and turned inward. Eyes look forward-left (Fig. 4-26).

Key to the movement: Keep the body erect, the arms remaining the ward-off force. The posture is opening movement, use the nose to exhale in it.

5. Continuing from previous movement. Turn the upper body slightly to the right. Move the center of the gravity leftward, both legs form a left bow step. At the same time, thread the left palm to the front of right side of chest with the arm twining adversely. Eyes look at the left palm (Fig. 4-27).

Fig. 4-26

Fig. 4-27

Key to the movement: Shifting the weight, the left knee doesn't surpassing the left tiptoes. Keep the shoulders relaxed and elbows lowered, use the nose to inhale.

6. Continuing from previous movement. Turn the upper body slightly to the left. Move the left palm leftward with the arm twining adversely, the lower the left elbow slightly with the arm twining

smoothly to the upside of left knee. Eyes follow the left hand, and then look forward (Fig. 4-28).

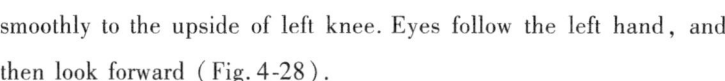

Key to the movement: The moving of the upper part of body and lower limbs must be coordinated. Keep the body erect, the top of head raised lightly in the mind, the shoulder relaxed and elbows lowered, use the nose to exhale in the movement.

Fig. 4-28

第五式 单 鞭

动作一:接上势身体微右转,两手双顺缠,左前右后旋转,手心朝上。重心在右,左腿以脚尖为轴,膝随身转里合,目视两手(图 4-23)。

要求:两手旋转时要圆活,不能有抽扯之形。此动吸气。

动作二:接上势,身体左转,重心在右,左腿以前脚掌着地,膝随身转外摆;右手逆缠,五指合拢,走弧线,腕向上提与肩平;左手心朝上,随身转下沉于腹前,左肘掤劲不丢,目视右手(图 4-24)。

要求:右手变勾手上提时,随身体旋转,塌腰,松肩,沉肘,以腰为轴,节节贯穿。此动为开,呼气。

动作三:接上势,身体右转,重心全移于右腿,左腿屈膝提起,左膝内扣;右手腕领劲,左手不动,松肩沉肘,上下相合,目视左前方(图 4-25)。

要求:右腿支撑重心,上下相合,切忌弯腰突臀。此动为合,吸气。

动作四:接上势,右腿支撑重心,左脚跟内侧着地,向左铲地滑出,脚尖上翘里合,右手腕领劲,左手下沉合劲,目视左前方(图 4-26)。

要求:立身中正,掤劲不丢。此动为开,呼气。

动作五:接上势,身体微右转,重心左移,成左弓步,左手穿掌上掤逆缠外翻至右胸前,目视前方,瞟视左手(图 4-27)。

要求:移重心时,裆走外下弧线,旋转移动,左膝不能超出左脚尖;左手外翻时,不能挑肩架肘。此动吸气。

动作六:接上势,身体微左转,左手逆缠外开至左膝上变顺缠放松下沉,目随左手送至体侧后,再转视正前方(图 4-28)。

要求:左脚尖外摆,右脚尖内扣,松胯屈膝,立身中正,虚领顶劲,松肩沉肘,两臂与两腿有上下相合之意。此动为外或内合,呼气。

Form 6　White Crane Spreads Its Wings

1. Continuing from previous movement. Turn the body to the left and move the toes of the left foot outward. Change the right hook-hand into a palm and cross the both palms in the front of chest with the arms

twining smoothly, the left palm facing rightward and fingers pointing upward, the right hand on the outside, the center of the right palm facing upward and fingers pointing the upper-front. Eyes look forward-right (Fig. 4-29).

Fig. 4-29

Fig. 4-30

2. Continuing from previous movement. Turn the body to the left. Move the center of gravity onto the left leg and take a step forward with the right foot. Move the right palm leftward slightly with the arm twining smoothly (Fig. 4-30).

3. Continuing from previous movement. Turn the upper body to the right, move the center of gravity rightward and take a step with the left foot to the forward-left of the right foot, only the toes touching the floor to form a left empty step. At the same time, press the left palm downward to upside of the left knee at the hip level, the left arm twining adversely and the center of the left palm facing downward. Move the

right palm upward and rightward in an arc, the right arm twining adversely and the center of right palm facing outward, the arms curved. Eyes look forward (Fig. 4-31, the side of Fig. 4-31).

Fig. 4-31

The side of fig. 4-31

第六式　白鹅亮翅

动作一:接上势,身体左转,左脚尖外摆,右手勾手变掌,双手顺缠交叉合于胸前,左手手指朝上,手心朝右;右手手心朝上,指尖朝前上,目视右前方(图4-29)。

动作二:接上势,身体左转,重心移到左腿,上右步,右手微顺缠加外掤劲(图4-30)。

动作三:接上势,身体右转,重心右移,两手同时逆缠外开,左手下按至左膝上方与胯平,手心朝下;右手上掤,手心朝外,两臂成半圆弧形。左脚上步收至右脚左前方,脚尖点地,目视前方(图 4-31、4-31 附图).

Form 7　Walk Obliquely

1. Continuing form previous movement. Turn the upper body to the left. Swing the left palm backward with the arm twining adversely, move the right palm forward and leftward in an arc with the arm twining smoothly. Eyes look to the forward-left (Fig. 4-32).

Fig. 4-32

Fig. 4-33

Key to the movement: Moving the palm, pay attention to that the waist serves as an axis in transporting the twining of the arms. Inhale in the movement.

2. Continuing form previous movement. Turn the body to the right.

Turn the toes of right foot outward and turn the left knee inward. While the turning of the body, move the left palm upward, rightward in an arc to the body at the nose level, the center of left palm facing rightward and fingers pointing upward. The right palm is pressed to beside the right thigh with the arm twining adversely and the palm facing downward. Eyes look to the forward-left (Fig. 4-33).

Key to the movement: Moving the both palms, pay attention to that the waist serves as an axis in transporting the arms. Use nose to exhale in the movement.

3. Continuing from previous movement. Move the center of gravity onto the right leg and lift the left leg with the knee bent. Ward off the both palms upward and rightward in arcs. Eyes look to the forward-left (Fig. 4-34).

Fig. 4-34

Fig. 4-35

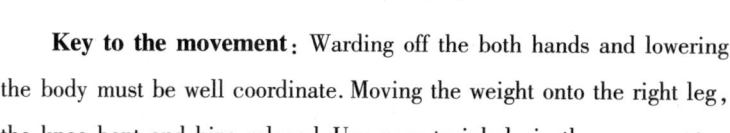

Key to the movement: Warding off the both hands and lowering the body must be well coordinate. Moving the weight onto the right leg, the knee bent and hips relaxed. Use nose to inhale in the movement.

4. Continuing from previous movement. Lower the body downward, take a step to the forward-left with the inside of left heel sliding on the floor, the toes hooked upward. Continue to ward off the both hands upward and rightward in arcs. Eyes look to the forward-left (Fig. 4-35).

Key to the movement: Stepping with the left foot and moving the both palms must be coordinated. The waist is relaxed. Use the nose to exhale in the movement.

5. Continuing from previous movement. Turn the body to the left and move the center of gravity leftward. Follow the turning of the body, move the left hand downward and leftward in an arc passing to the front of the left knee, the left arm twining adversely. The right hand moves upward and leftward in an arc to under the right ear. Eyes look to the forward-left (Fig. 4-36).

Fig. 4-36

Key to the movement: Turning the body and shifting the weight must be well coordinated.

6. Continuing from previous movement. Continue to turn the body

to the left. The left hand is changed into a hook—hand and raised upward and leftward in an arc to in the front of left side of the chest, the left hand at the shoulder level. The right hand moves leftward to in the front of the chest, the center of the palm facing leftward and the fingers pointing upward. Eyes look forward (Fig. 4-37).

Fig. 4-37

Key to the movement: Raising the left hand, the power is focused at the tip of the hook-hand.

7. Continuing from previous movement. Turn the body to the right, move the right palm leftward, forward and rightward in a plane arc passing to the front of chest, lowering the shoulders and elbows downward, and bending knees and relaxing hips. Eyes look forward (Fig. 4-38).

Fig. 4-38

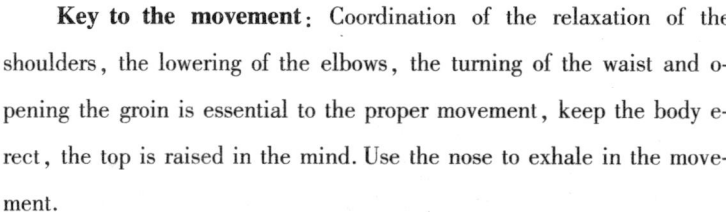

Key to the movement: Coordination of the relaxation of the shoulders, the lowering of the elbows, the turning of the waist and opening the groin is essential to the proper movement, keep the body erect, the top is raised in the mind. Use the nose to exhale in the movement.

第七式　斜　　行

动作一:接上势,脚步不动,身体左转,左手逆缠后摆;右手顺缠,松肩沉肘,向左前划弧摆动,目视左前方(图 4-32)。

要求:以身带手,催动两臂转动,如风摆杨柳一样。此动吸气。

动作二:接上势,身体右转,右脚尖右摆,左脚尖着地,左膝里合;左手随转身由左后向右上划弧,合于鼻前中线,立掌,掌心朝右;右手逆缠划弧下按于右腿外侧,手心朝下,目视左前方(图 4-33)。

要求:两手转动时,以腰为轴,顶劲领起。此动呼气。

动作三:接上势,重心移至右腿,左腿屈膝提起,两手向右上掤,目视身体左前方(图 4-34)。

要求:两手上掤,身体下沉,右腿支撑重心,屈膝松胯,上下相合。此动吸气。

动作四:接上势,身体下沉,左脚跟内侧着地向左前方开步,脚尖上翘,两手继续上掤,目视身体左前方(图 4-35)。

要求:开步时,两手上掤,腰劲下塌,上下对称。此动呼气。

动作五:接上势,身体左转,重心左移,左手逆缠,随身体左转走下弧至左膝下;右手顺缠向后环绕变逆缠合于右耳下,目视左前方(图 4-36)。

要求:转体与移重心要协调一致。

动作六:接上势,身体继续左转,重心在左,左手五指合拢变勾手,弧线上提至肩平,右手立掌合于胸前,目视前方(图4-37)。

要求:左手上提,手腕放松领劲。

动作七:接上势,身体右转,右手逆缠划弧向右拉开,松肩沉肘,含胸塌腰,松胯屈膝,目视前方(图4-38)。

要求:此势两手两足位四隅角,要立身中正,舒展大方,开裆贵圆,虚领顶劲,上下四傍,八面支撑,谓之"中定身法"。此动呼气。

Form 8 Brush knee

1. Continuing from previous movement. Lower the body down, relax the hips and bend the knees to squat. At the same time, change the left hook-hand into a palm and rotate both arms outward while moving both palms downward and inward in arcs and closing them in the upside of the left knee. Eyes look to the lower—front (Fig. 4-39).

Key to the movement: Closing the both hands and lowering the body must be well coordinated, keep the body erect.

2. Continuing from previous movement. Close both hands inward and raise them upward to the chest level, the fingers of both palms pointing upward. At the same time, move the weight onto the right leg and withdraw the left foot backward, only the toes landing on the floor to form a left empty step, the left knee bent and the

hips relaxed. Eyes look forward (Fig. 4-40).

Key to the movement: Shifting the weight onto the leg and withdrawing the left foot backward should be natural. Use the nose to inhale in the movement.

Fig. 4-39

Fig. 4-40

第八式　搂　　膝

动作一:接上势,身体下沉,松胯屈膝下蹲;两手先逆后顺略上领,再变顺缠下合于左膝上方,重心在左腿,目视前下方(图 4-39)。

要求:两手下合时,要身法正直,随身下沉,两手如捧水一样合劲不丢。此动先吸气后呼气。

动作二:接上势,两手领劲上掤,左手在前,右手在后,立掌于胸前中线,随手上领,重心移至右腿;左脚收回至右脚左前方,脚尖点地,屈膝松胯,目视前方(图4-40)。

要求:重心走下弧后移至右腿,左腿收回要自然。此动吸气。

Form 9 Twist step

1. Continuing from previous movement. Turn the upper body to the right slightly, move the center of gravity onto the right leg and lift the left leg upward with the knee bent. At the same time, deflect both palms downward and rightward in arcs with the left arm twining smoothly and the right arm twining adversely. Eyes look forward (Fig. 4-41).

Fig. 4-41

Fig. 4-42

Key to the movement: Closing power of the upper and lower parts of the body during lifting knee is required in order achieve stability while standing on one leg. Use the nose to exhale in the movement.

2. Continuing from previous movement. Turn the body to the left slightly. Step forward with the right foot landing the heel on the floor and toes hooked upward. At the same time, move the both palms upward and forward in arcs with the left arm twining adversely and the right arm twining smoothly. Eyes look forward (Fig. 4-42).

Key to the movement: Stepping forward with the left foot and moving the both palms must be well coordinated. Use the nose to inhale fist and then exhale in the movement.

3. Continuing from previous movement. Turn the body to the left, move the weight onto the left leg. Press the left palm downward with the left arm twining adversely and push the right palm forward with the right arm twining adversely. At the same time, lift the right leg with the knee bent. Eyes look forward (Fig. 4-43).

Key to the movement: The footwork is light. Use the nose to inhale in the movement.

4. Continuing from previous movement. Step forward with the right foot heel land on the floor, the toes hooked upward. Turn the body to the left slightly, lower the left palm and push the right palm forward. Eyes look forward (Fig. 4-44).

Key to the movement: The footwork is light and continued described by such phrases as "Walk the steps of a cat, the footwork is light" in the boxing theory.

Fig. 4-43

Fig. 4-44

5. Continuing from previous movement. Turn the toes of right foot outward, move the weight onto the right leg, lift the left leg and step to the forward—left with the left foot. Turn the body rightward about go degrees, lower the right palm lightly with the arm twining adversely, move the left palm upward, rightward and downward in an arc passing to the ear, and cross both hands at the

Fig. 4-45

wrists in the front of chest. Eyes look forward (Fig. 4-45).

Key to the movement: Pushing palms and stepping forward must be well coordinated, the body erect, the arms bent slightly. The movement is continued with the previous movement, use the nose to inhale fist and then exhale during it.

第九式　拗　　步

动作一:接上式,身体微右转,两手右逆缠左顺缠后下攦,左腿屈膝提起,重心在右腿,目视前方(图 4-41)。

要求:下攦时掤劲不丢,提腿上下相合,右腿要稳。此动呼气。

动作二:接上式,身体微左转,右腿向前上步,脚跟着地,脚尖上翘,重心在右腿;同时两手左逆右顺缠,向上向前掤,目视前方(图 4-42)。

要求:向前迈步要自然,两手划弧上掤下攦,要与身法自然结合。两手上翻时吸气,下沉时呼气。

动作三:接上势,身体左转,重心移至左腿,左手逆缠下按,右手逆缠向前推出;右腿屈膝提起,目视前方(图 4-43)。

要求:步法稳重,上步轻灵自然。此动先呼气后吸气。

动作四:接上势,右脚向前上步,脚跟着地,脚尖上翘,重心在左腿,身体微左转,左手下沉,右手前推,目视前方(图 4-44)。

要求:上步如猫行,轻灵自然。

动作五:接上势,右脚尖外摆,重心移至右腿,提左脚向左前方上一步;身体随上步自左向右转体 90 度;右手逆缠下沉,左手顺缠上翻划弧经左耳变逆缠,与右手交叉相合于胸前,重心偏右腿,目视前方(图4-45)。

要求:移重心上步时,身体不能上提,两手交叉,掤劲撑圆,立身中正。此动接上势,先吸气后呼气。

Form 10 Cover Hands and Strike with Arm

1. Continuing from previous movement. Turn the body to the right slightly and move the center of gravity to the left. At the same time, separate the both hands downward to respective sides in arcs with the arms twining adversely. Eyes look forward (Fig. 4-46).

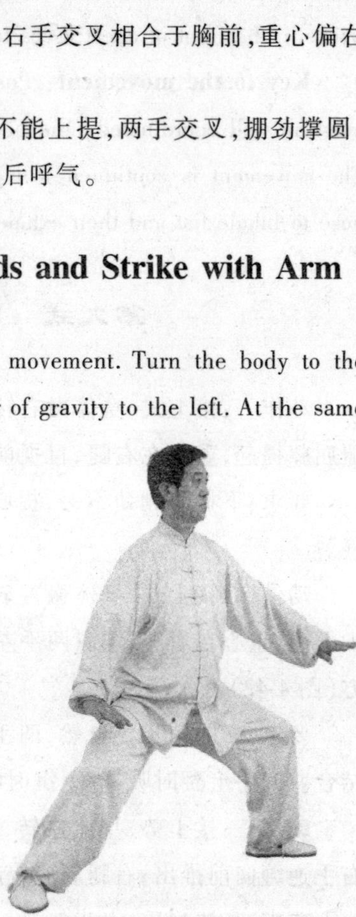

Fig. 4-46

Key to the movement: In separating the hands to respective sides, using the waist to transport the arms, continue to inhale in the movement.

2. Continuing from previous movement. Turn the body to the left and shift the weight rightward slightly. At the same time, move the right hand rightward and inward in an arc, change the right palm into a fist and withdraw it to the right side of the waist with the center of fist facing upward. Move the left palm to in the

front of the chest with the center of the palm facing rightward and the fingers pointing upward. Eyes look forward (Fig. 4-47).

Fig. 4-47

Key to the movement: Coordination of closing the hands, relaxing the waist, lowering the hips and bending knees is essential for mustering of the whole force. Continue to inhale in the movement.

3. Continuing from previous movement. Turn the body suddenly to the left and strike the right fist power fully to the forward—right at the shoulder level with the arm twining adversely, butt the left elbow backward. Eyes look at the right fist (Fig. 4-48).

Fig. 4-48

Key to the movement: Application of power is quickly, the waist is twisted, the groin turned and the left hip is relaxed.

Thrusting the right fist forward and butting the left elbow backward must be well coordinated.

第十式　掩手肱拳

动作一：接上势，身体略右转，重心左移，两手逆缠自下向左右分开，目视前方（图 4-46）。

要求：两手分时，以身带手，沉稳圆活，此动接上势，继续吸气。

动作二：接上势，重心右移，身体略左转，右手顺缠上翻变拳合于右腰间，拳心向上；左手由逆缠变顺缠，立掌合于胸前正中线，目视前方（图 4-47）。

要求：握拳合劲时身体中正下沉，松胯屈膝，劲合于右腿，蓄劲待发。此动吸气。

动作三：接上势，右腿蹬地里合，身体迅速左转，松左胯，右拳逆缠螺旋前冲，左肘向后发劲，目视右拳前方（图 4-48）。

要求：发劲时，拧腰转裆，将右拳突然冲出，前拳后肘，对称发力，完整一气。

Form 11　Pat High on the Horse

1. Turn the body to the right, change both fists into palms, move the left palm forward and upward in an arc with the arm twining adversely, move the right palm downward with the arm twining adversely. Eyes look forward (Fig. 4-49).

Key to the movement: Separating both hands to respective sides and turning the body to the right must be well coordinated. Keep the body erect, the both arms bent slightly and remain the warding—off force. Use the nose to exhale in the movement.

Fig. 4-49

2. Continuing from previous movement. Turn the body to the left and shift the weight rightward, the toes of the right foot turned inward. Turn the left arm outward so that the left palm faces upward. Move the right palm backward and upward in an arc to the shoulder level, and then withdraw it to in the front of the right shoulder. Eyes follow the right hand then look to the forward—left (Fig. 4-50).

Fig. 4-50

Key to the move-

ment: Swinging the right hand, the chest opened, the hips relaxed. Use the nose to inhale in the movement.

3. Continuing from previous movement: Turn the body to the left and shift the center of gravity onto the right leg, pull the left foot to the inside of the right ankle, left toes touching the floor. At the same time, push the right palm rightward and withdraw the left palm backward to in the front of abdomen at the navel level, the center of the palm facing upward. Eyes look to forward—right (Fig. 4-51, the side of Fig. 4-51).

Fig. 4-51

The side of fig. 4-51

Key to the movement: Pushing the right palm must be coordinated with the turning of body. Use the nose to exhale in the movement.

第十一式　高　探　马

动作一:接上势,重心不变,身体右转,两拳变掌,左手逆缠前掤,右手逆缠下分,目视前方(图 4-49)。

要求:手臂分开时,随裆腰旋转,身法中正,两臂掤劲不丢,有支撑八面之势。呼气。

动作二:接上势,身体左转,重心右移,右脚尖内扣;右手顺缠外翻至身体右侧与肩平,再变逆缠合于右肩前,左手顺缠里合。目随右手旋转,再视左前方(图 4-50)。

要求:右手外翻上掤旋转时,要开胸松胯,有开中寓合之势,此动吸气。

动作三:接上势,身体左转,重心在右腿,左脚向左后划弧,收于右脚内侧,脚尖点地;同时右臂松肩沉肘,顺缠向右侧推;左手顺缠收至腹前与脐平,手心向上,目视右前方(图 4-51、4-51 附图)。

要求:推右掌要随转体,周身一致。此动呼气。

Form 12　Kick with The Left Heel

1. Continuing from previous movement. Move the right palm slightly inward and then, separate both palms to respective sides, the palms facing outward and fingers pointing upward. At the same time, shift the weight of the body onto the left leg and step rightward with the right foot (Fig. 4-52).

2. Continuing from previous movement. Clench the both palms into fists, move them inward and cross them in the front of abdomen, the centers of fists facing inward. At the same time, lift the left leg with the knee bent, the toes of the foot pointing downward naturally. Eyes look to the forward—left (Fig. 4-53, the side of Fig. 4-53).

Fig. 4-52

Fig. 4-53

The side of fig. 4-53

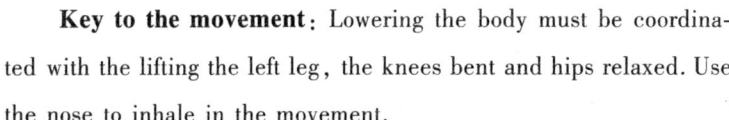

Key to the movement: Lowering the body must be coordinated with the lifting the left leg, the knees bent and hips relaxed. Use the nose to inhale in the movement.

3. Continuing from previous movement. Shift the center of gravity onto the right leg, the upper body leans rightward slightly, kick the left foot to the upper-left at the waist level, the knee being extended from its flexed posture, the outer edge of the foot serving as force point. At the same time, thrust the both fists to their respective sides of the body, the fists are at shoulder level, the force is focused at the knuckles (Fig. 4-54).

Fig. 4-54

Key to the movement: Kicking the left foot and thrusting with both fists must be well coordinated. Keep standing on the right leg steady. Use nose to exhale in the movement.

第十二式　左蹬一根

动作一:接上势,左手逆缠外挪,右手先顺缠略里合再逆缠与左手同时外挪,两手心均朝外;同时,重心移到左腿,提右腿向右横开一步(图 4-52)。

动作二:接上势,两手轻握拳,顺缠里合于腹前,拳心向里;同时,左腿屈膝提起,脚尖放松,悬于裆内,目视左前方(图 4-53、4-53 附图)。

要求:身体下沉,提腿,屈膝松胯,上下相合,两肘外挪,蓄而待发。此动吸气。

动作三:接上势,右腿支撑重心,身体略右倾,左脚用腰裆弹力向左侧平蹬与腰平。两拳分别向左右冲击,力贯拳面(图 4-54)。

要求:右腿支撑要稳,左脚和左右拳要同时发劲,要"缩身如猬形,吐气贯长虹"。此动呼气。

Form 13　Jade Girl Works at Shuttles

1. Continuing from previous movement. The left foot lands on the floor. At the same time, change the both fists into palms and cross them to in to front of abdomen with the arms twining smoothly (Fig. 4-55).

2. Continuing form previous movement. Turn the body to the

right, the left toes turned inward. Shift the center of gravity to the left. Turn the right knee outward using the toes of right foot as an axis. Following the turning of the body, move the both palms rightward to in the front of chest with the fingers of both palms pointing upward, the left palm is placed on the inside of the right forearm. Eyes look forward (Fig. 4-56).

Fig. 4-55

Fig. 4-56

Key to the movement: In turning of the body, pay attention to that the waist as an axis to initiate the shoulder, elbows then palms. Use the nose to inhale and then exhale in the movement.

3. Continuing from previous movement. Bend the knees and relax the hips to lower the body, close the both palms downward with the both arms twining adversely. Eyes look forward (Fig. 4-57).

Fig. 4-57

Fig. 4-58

Key to the movement: Lowering the body and pressing the both palms downward, don't bend the upper body forward. Continue to exhale in the movement.

4. Continuing from previous movement. The right and left feet jump up in succession from the floor and raise the both palm upward quickly with the arms twining smoothly. Eyes look forward (Fig. 4-58).

Key to the movement: Raising the palms upward, the powers are focused at the both palms. The movement of jumping should be lightly. Use the nose to exhale in the movement.

5. Continuing from previous movement. Stamp on the floor with the left and right feet in quick succession, simultaneously pressing both palms downward with the arms twining adversely. Eyes look

forward (Fig. 4-59).

Fig. 4-59

Fig. 4-60

Key to the movement: The left and right foot stamp successively and forcefully, keep the body erect. Use the nose to exhale in the movement.

6. Continuing from previous movement. Raise the both palms up with arms twining adversely and lift the right leg upward with the knee bent. Eyes look forward (Fig. 4-60).

Key to the movement: Raising the both palms upward and lifting the right leg must be well—coordinated. The entire body is erect and steady. Use the nose to inhale in the movement.

7. Continuing from previous movement. Shift the center of gravity onto the left leg. Turn the body leftward, kick the right foot

quickly to the forward-right. At the same time, push the right palm forward-right with the arm twining adversely and butt the left elbow rear-left with the arm twining adversely. Eyes look to the forward-right (Fig. 4-61).

Fig. 4-61

Key to the movement: The application power should be quick and forceful. Balance must be steady and the body upright. Use the nose to exhale in the movement.

8. Continuing from previous movement. Step to the forward-right with the right foot, move the center of gravity to the right leg. Turn the body slightly to the right and lower the left palm slightly. Eyes look forward (Fig. 4-62).

Fig. 4-62

Key to the movement: The position is transition

movement. After landing the right foot on the floor, lift it quickly to continue next movement. Use the nose to inhale fist and exhale in the movement.

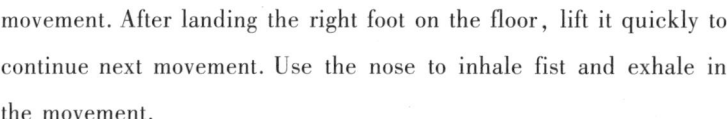

9. Continuing from previous movement. The left foot swings forward and the right foot jumps up forcefully so the body is turned rightward about 180 degrees in the air, the left palm pushing leftward and the right palm blocking to the upper-right of the head. The left foot lands on the floor and the right foot inserts a step to the rear—left behind the left with the right heel raised from the floor. Eyes look leftward (Fig. 4-63).

Fig. 4-63

Fig. 4-64

Key to the movement: The position is a transition posture for next one. The footwork is light. Keep the body erect.

10. Continuing from previous movement. Turn the left leg in-

ward by using the heel as a pivot and the heel of the right foot leftward by using the ball of the foot as a pivot as the body is turned rightward 180 degrees. Shift the center onto the right leg. At the same time, deflect both palms to the rear-left. Eyes look to the forward-left (Fig. 4-64).

Key to the movement: The previous movements should be linked compactly, smoothly and without interruption.

第十三式　玉女穿梭

动作一:接上势,左脚落地,两拳变掌顺缠合于腹前(图 4-55)。

动作二:接上势,重心左移,身体右转,两手随之右转掤于胸前,立掌,右手在前,左手在后,同时右脚以脚尖为轴右膝外摆,左脚尖内扣随身右转。目视前方(图 4-56)。

要求:转身时要以腰催肩,以肩催肘,掤于手。此动先吸气后呼气。

动作三:接上势,屈膝松胯,身体下沉,两手双逆缠下合,目视前方(图 4-57)。

要求:随身体下沉,两手下按,切勿弯腰。此动接上势下沉呼气。

动作四:接上势,两手顺缠迅速向上领起,双脚随之上纵离地,目视前方(图 4-58)。

要求:以手领劲,周身一致,上纵轻灵。此动吸气。

动作五:接上势,双震脚落地,双手逆缠随之下按,目视前方

(图 4-59)。

要求:震脚落地,两手下按要沉重有力,完整一气,立身中正。此动呼气。

动作六:接上势,两手逆缠上掤,右腿随之屈膝提起,目视前方(图 4-60)。

要求:手掤提腿,立身稳重,周身合一,内劲团聚不散。此动吸气。

动作七:接上势,重心在左腿,身体迅速左转,右腿里合外蹬,右掌逆缠前推,左手逆缠,向左后发肘劲,目视右前方(图 4-61)。

要求:将周身团聚之劲,迅速贯于右脚、右手和左肘,左腿独立稳重。此动呼气。

动作八:接上势,右脚跨步落地,重心移至右腿,身体微右转,左掌略下沉,目视前方(图 4-62)。

要求:此势为窜跳的过渡动作,右脚落地即起,用右脚前掌弹地蹬起前跃,此动先吸气后呼气。

动作九:接上势,右脚蹬地弹起前纵,身体在空中向右旋转 180 度,左手逆缠向左猛推,右掌向右开;左脚先落地,右脚从左脚后插过,脚尖着地,目视左侧(图 4-63)。

要求:此势为下势过渡动作,练习时可以不停,落地轻稳,身法中正。

动作十:接上势,身体右转 180 度,重心移至右腿,左腿随转身里合;同时,两手随转体左顺右逆由左向右后转搬,目视左前方(图 4-64)。

要求:转身时,身法下沉,两手掤劲不丢。此动吸气。

Form 14 Wave Hands Like Clouds

1. Continuing from previous movement. Move the right palm rightward, downward and leftward in an arc to in the front of abdomen, the right arm twining smoothly, the center of right palm facing leftward, the left arm twining adversely, the center of left palm facing outward. At the same time, take a step to the rear—right with the left foot, the toes landing on the floor (Fig. 4-65).

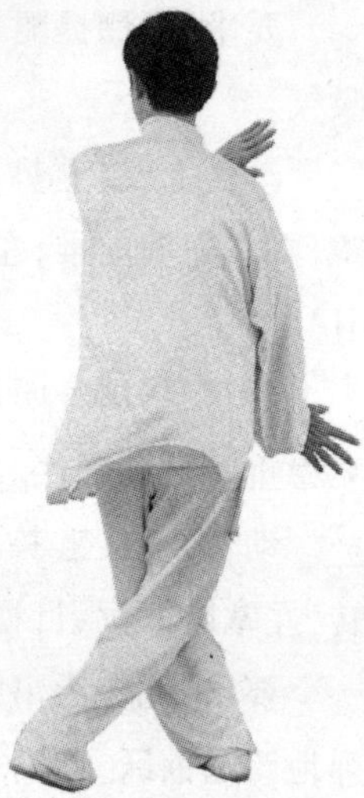

Fig. 4-65

2. Continuing from previous movement. Turn the body slightly to the right and shift the weight onto the right leg. The sole is flat on the floor. The left foot moves a step to the left, the heel landing on the floor, the tiptoes of foot hooked upward. At the same time, move the right palm upward and rightward in an arc with the arm twining adversely and move the left palm leftward, downward and leftward in an arc to the front of abdomen with the arm twining smoothly. Eyes look to the forward-left (Fig. 4-66).

3. Continuing from previous movement. Turn the body slightly to the right, move the left palm rightward, upward and leftward in an arc, the left arm with twining adversely. Move the right palm

rightward, downward and leftward in an arc to in the front of the abdomen, the right arm with twining smootly. At the same time, shift the weight onto the left leg, take a step to the rear-left of left foot with the right foot. Eyes look forward-left (Fig. 4-67).

Fig. 4-66

Fig. 4-67

Key to the movement: Pay attention to that the waist serves as an axis to initiate the movements of the arms. The go round and begin, moving three steps continuously.

第十四式 云 手

动作一:接上势,右手顺缠里合于腹前,掌心向左,左手逆缠里合外掤于左肩前,掌心向外;同时,左脚向右后插步,脚尖点地(图 4-65)。

动作二:接上势,身体微右转,重心移至右腿,右脚踏实,提左腿向左前方横开一步,脚跟着地,脚尖上翘;同时,右手逆缠外翻上掤,左手顺缠走下弧,里合于腹前。目视左前方(图 4-66)。

动作三:接上势,身体微右转,左手由顺缠变逆缠,划弧外翻上掤,右手变顺缠里合于腹前;同时,重心移至左腿,右脚插步于左脚左后方,目视左前方(图 4-67)。

要求:云手以腰为轴,两手在体前分别向左右两侧划弧,如车轮滚翻,上下往返。开一插一为一步,共 4 步,也可根据场地灵活掌握。

Form 15 Turn Body with Lotus Kick

1. Turn the body to the rear—right about 180 degrees using the left heel and then right heel as pivots. At the same time, deflect the both palms to the rear—right, the right palm moves to in the front of the chest with the right arm twining adversely, the palm facing obliquely upward. Move the left palm to in the front of the left shoulder with the arm twining smoothly, the palm facing upward. Eyes look forward—left (Fig. 4-68).

Fig. 4-68

Fig. 4-69 Fig. 4-70

2. Continuing from previous movement. Shift the weight onto the right leg as the body turns slightly to the right, lift the left leg with knees bent, and then take a step to the forward—left with the left foot. At the same time, deflect the both palms to the rear—right. Eyes look forward (Fig. 4-69).

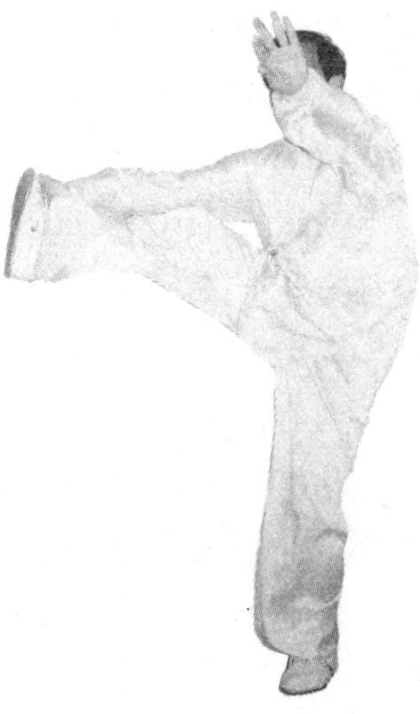

Fig. 4-71

3. Continuing from previous movement. Shift the weight leftward as the upper body turns to the right. At the same time, deflect both palms downward and leftward in

arcs to the right side of the body. Eyes look at both palms (Fig. 4-70).

4. Continue from previous movement. Shift the weight onto the left leg, swing and kick the right foot upward and rightward in an arc. The left and right palms slap successively on the outside of the right foot. Eyes look forward (Fig. 4-71).

Key to the movement: The swinging leg and slapping foot movements should be quick. Inhale first and then exhale during the movement.

第十五式　转身双摆莲

动作一:接上势,两手左顺右逆缠向右后方搌;身体先以左脚跟为轴,再以右脚跟为轴向右后旋转 180 度。右手位于胸前中线,掌心朝右上方,左手拉于左肩前,掌心向上,目视左前方(图 4-68)。

动作二:接上势,重心右移,身体微右转,左腿屈膝提起,向左前方开步;两手向右后方捌,目视前方(图 4-69)。

动作三:接上势,身体向右转,重心左移,两手由后搌转为走下弧向前合劲,合于右腰侧,目视前方(图 4-70)。

动作四:接上势,重心在左腿,提右腿向左走下弧向上,再向右摆击,两手掌向前与右脚外侧击拍相合,目视前方(图 4-71)。

要求:摆脚与手合击的速度要快,劲力完整一气,此动先吸气后呼气。

Form 16 Strike Face Like Canon

1. Continuing previous movement. After swing leg outward, the right foot falls down to the rear—right, the weight is still on the left leg. At the same time, ward off the both palms to the upper—left. Eyes look forward (Fig. 4-72).

Fig. 4-72

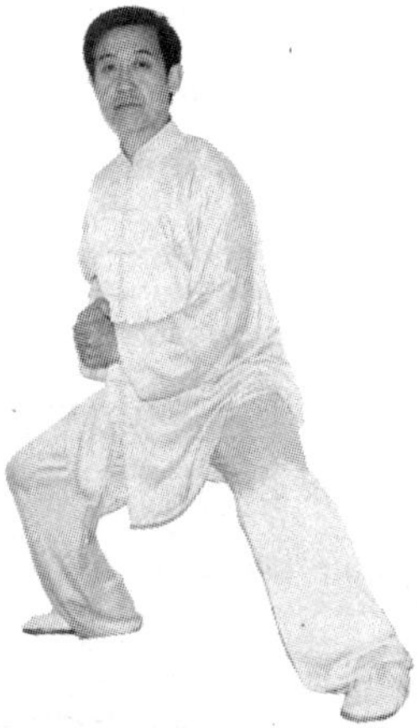

Fig. 4-73

Key to the movement: The entire movement should be completed continuously. Inhale during the movement.

2. Continuing previous movement. Turn the body slightly to the right, the weight shifting to the right leg. At the same time, deflect both palms downward and rightward to in the front of the right chest, clenching the fingers of both hands into fists. Eyes look forward-left (Fig. 4-73).

Key to the movement: Deflecting both palms, shifting the weight to right leg and turning the body to the right should be coordinated, the upper body must be not bent forward. Exhale first then inhale in the movement.

Fig. 4-74

3. Continuing from previous movement. Turn the body to the left and shift the weight quickly to the left leg. At the same time, punch the both fists forward with eyes of fists facing upward and the centers of fists facing each other. Eyes look forward (Fig. 4-74).

Key to the movement: While applying power, bend the knees, sink the hips, turn the waist and punch the fists quickly, concentrate power at the faces of fists. Exhale in the movement.

第十六式　当　头　炮

动作一:接上势,拍脚后,右腿向右后撤一步,两手逆缠向左上掤,重心在左腿,目视前方(图 4-72)。

要求:拍脚后步要稳,上引下进协调一致。此动吸气。

动作二:接上势,身体微右转,重心移至右腿;同时,两手左顺右逆缠随重心后移下搌再变拳合于右胸侧,目视左前方(图 4-73)。

要求:两手下搌,随重心移动转身一致,切勿弯腰。此动先呼气后吸气。

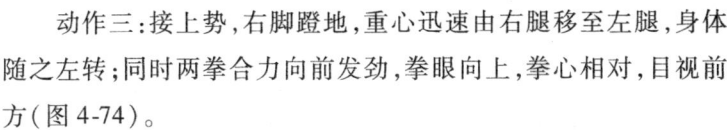

动作三:接上势,右脚蹬地,重心迅速由右腿移至左腿,身体随之左转;同时两拳合力向前发劲,拳眼向上,拳心相对,目视前方(图4-74)。

要求:心意一动,猝然抖发,如金狮抖毛,猛虎下山,完全是腰裆的弹抖劲,力贯拳顶。此动呼气。

Form 17 Buddha's Warrior Attendant Pounds Mortar

1. Continuing from previous movement. Change the both fists into both palms, deflect them rightward and backward in arcs with the left arm twining smoothly and right arm twining adversely. At the same time, move the center of gravity to the right. Eyes look forward—left (Fig. 4-75).

2. Continuing from previous movement. Move the weight leftward as the sole of the left foot is placed on the floor. Turn the body leftward 45 degrees. The left palm moves downward and leftward in an arc to in the front of the chest, the elbow bent, the palm facing downward. Move the right palm rightward and downward in an arc to beside the right knee, the palm facing obliquely downward. Eyes look forward

Fig. 4-75

(Fig. 4-76、77).

Fig. 4-76

Fig. 4-77

3. Continuing from previous movement. The right palm performs an uppercut in an upward and forward arc to in the front of chest with palm facing upward. The left palm describes a forward curve and is then placed on the right forearm, palm facing downward. At the same time, turn the body to the left and step with the right foot to in the front of the left foot only the toes landing on the floor to form a right empty step, the weight is onto the left leg. Eyes look forward (Fig. 4-78).

4. Continuing from previous movement. Lower the left palm to in front of the abdomen with the arm twining smoothly, the palm facing upward, simultaneously clench the fingers of the right hand in-

to a fist and lower it downward onto the center of the left palm, the center of fist facing upward. Eyes look forward (Fig. 4-79).

Fig. 4-78

Fig. 4-79

5. Continuing from previous movement. Raise the right fist up to shoulder level with the arm twining adversely, elbow bent and the center of fist facing inward. At the same time, lift the right leg with knee bent and toes pointing downward naturally. Eyes look forward (Fig. 4-80).

6. Continuing from previous movement. Stamp the right foot on the floor about shoulder—width apart to inside of the left foot, the entire sole touching on the floor. At the same time, smash the right fist downward onto the left palm with the arm twining smoothly, the elbows bent slightly, the arms cured in semicircle. Eyes look forward (Fig. 4-81).

Fig. 4-80

Fig. 4-81

第十七式　金刚捣碓

动作一：接上势，两拳变掌左顺右逆向右后上方掤带，同时重心由左向右移，目视左前方（图 4-75）。

动作二：接上势，重心由右腿移至左腿，左脚尖外摆踏实，身体随重心移动向左转 45 度；两手左逆右顺缠走下弧向前掤，左手掤至胸前，手心朝下，右手下沉至右膝内上方，手心朝外，指尖朝后，目视前方（图 4-76、4-77）。

动作三：接上势，左手向前撩掌，向上再向内环绕合于胸前右小臂内侧；同时，右手领右脚弧线向前上托掌合于右胸前与左手相合。右手心朝上，左手心朝下；右脚经左脚内侧向前上步，脚尖点地，重心在左腿，目视前方（图 4-78）。

动作四:接上势,左手顺缠外翻下沉于腹前,手心朝上;右手握拳下沉落于左掌心内,拳心朝上。目视前方(图4-79)。

动作五:接上势,右拳逆缠向上提起与肩平,右腿屈膝松胯提起,右脚悬于裆内,脚尖自然下垂,目视前方(图4-80)。

动作六:接上势,右脚震脚落地,脚掌踏平,两脚间距同肩宽;右拳顺缠下沉落于左掌心内,两臂撑圆,目视前方(图4-81)。

Form 18 Finishing Form

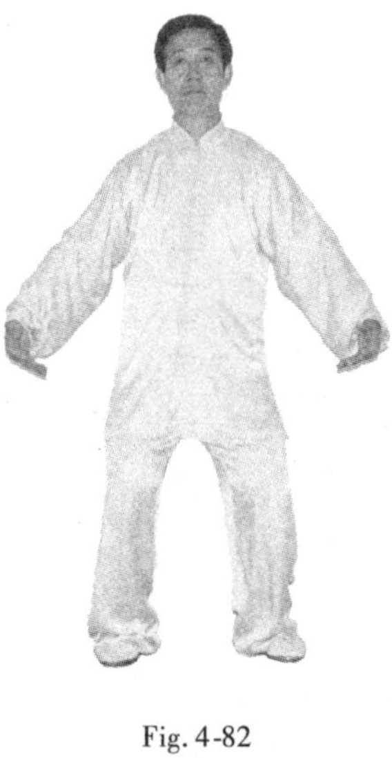

Fig. 4-82

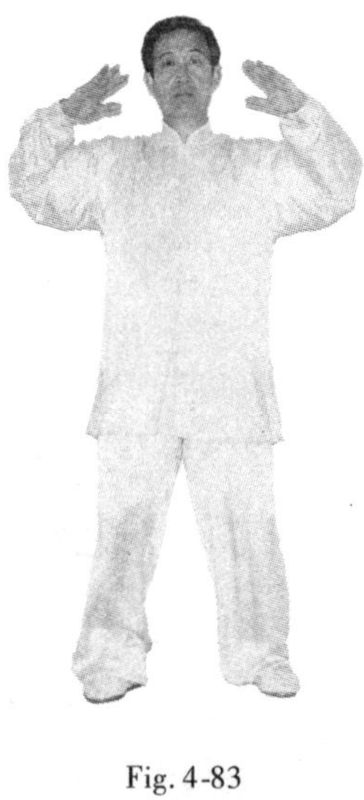

Fig. 4-83

1. Continuing from previous movement. Open the right fist into a palm and move the both palms downward and sideways to the sides of the body. At the same time, lower the body downward and bend the knees slightly and relax the hips. Eyes look forward (Fig. 4-82).

Key to the movement: While separating the palms and lowering the body, the upper body must be not bent forward. Inhale first and then exhale in the movement.

2. Separate the both palms sideways to respective sides of the body, and move them upward, inward and downward in arcs to the front of shoulders. Eyes look forward (Fig. 4-83).

Key to the movement: While raising the palms upward, the muscle of chest, back and abdomen relaxed, the shoulder relaxed and the elbows lowered. Exhale in the movement.

3. Continuing from previous movement. Press slowly the both palms to the sides of the thighs. Eyes look forward (Fig. 4-84).

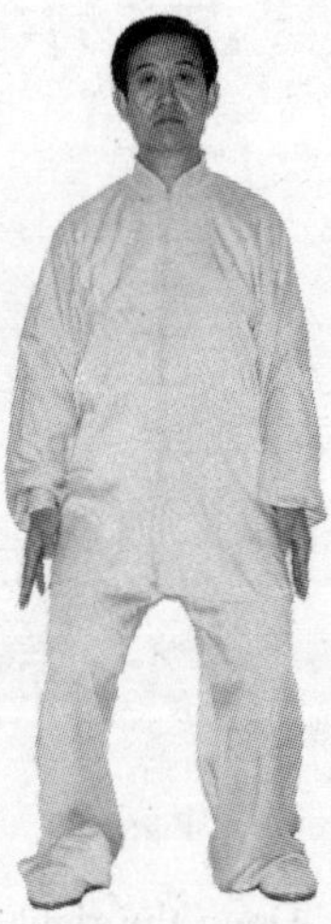

Fig. 4-84

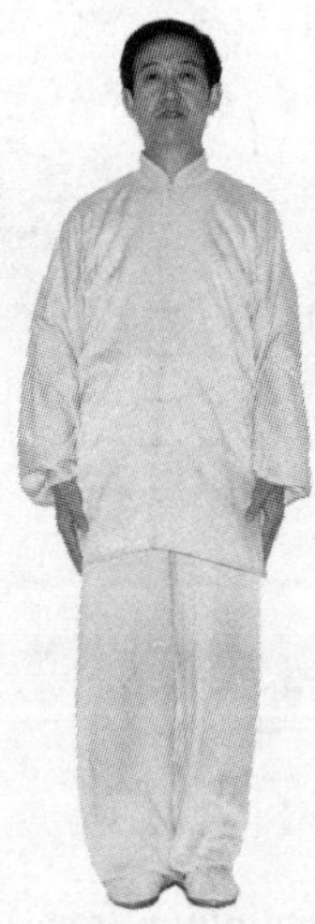

Fig. 4-85

Key to the movement: While pressing the palms downward use the nose to exhale, the entire body relaxed, the vigor flowing to

Dantian.

4. Continuing from previous movement. Slowly raise the body and stand upward, lower the both palms downward, natural hanging them at the side of the thighs. Then draw the left foot inward to the inside of the right foot with feet together at attention. Eyes look straight ahead (Fig. 4-85).

第十八式　收　　势

动作一:接上势,右拳变掌,两手向左右下分,身微下沉,屈膝松胯,目视前方(图 4-82)。

要求:两手分,身下沉,切勿弯腰。此动先吸气后呼气。

动作二:两手同时各向左右划外弧合于两肩前,目视前方(图 4-83)。

要求:两手上升,松肩沉肘,胸、腹、背各部肌肉均松弛下沉。此动吸气。

动作三:接上势,两手顺身体两侧缓缓下按于两大腿外侧,目视前方(图 4-84)。

要求:两手下按,呼气,周身放松,气归丹田,意形归原。一套拳练完,心平气和,自始至终,一气贯通。

动作四:接上势,身体慢慢立起,恢复到自然站立姿势,目视前方(图 4-85)。

A BRIEF BIOGRAPHY OF CHEN ZHENGLEI

Chen Zhenglei was born May 1949 in the place of origin of Taijiquan, Chenjiagou Village, in Wenxian, Henan Province. Master Chen, of the 19th generation of Chen family, is the 11th generation direct-line successor of Chen Style Taijiquan, Head Coach of Wenxian Chenjiagou Taijiquan Promotion Center, that of Henan Taiji Physical Fitness Co. Ltd; is now, at the same time, Vice Director of Henan Martial Arts Administration, Vice Chairman of Henan Martial Arts Association, Instructor of national social physical training, Committee Member of China Physical Culture Science Institute, one of the "10 Top Martial Arts Masters" of present China.

From the age of eight, he studied Taijiquan under the tutelage of his two uncles, Chen Zhaopi, a famous instructor at the Naijing Martial Arts Academy, and Chen Zhaokui, the son of Chen Fake. For over 30 years, he has practiced assiduously and achieved marvelous skill; because of this, he is known as an Outstanding Master of Taijiquan" and enjoys a high reputation in China and abroad.

From 1974 to 1987, he won in succession over 10 gold medals at the Henan Province Martial Arts Competition, winning the competition on numerous occasions. He has also successfully defended his title as Grand Champion of Taijiquan at two successive National Taijiquan Competitions. In 1983, he was appointed as a coach at the Henan Province Martial Arts Academy. In 1987, he was appointed as a National Level First Class Martial Arts Judge. At the 1988 China-Japan Taijiquan Competition, he came in first place. From 1988 to 1989, the team he coached won three team first places in the Taijiquan, Taiji Sword, and pushhands competitions at Henan Province and National Martial Arts Meets. Individually, the competitors that he coached won 15 individual gold and 12 individual silver medals.

Putting his spare time to good use, Chen Zhenglei has written books, articles and reports, such as: Compendium of Taiji Boxing and Weapons (Chenshi Taijiquan Xie Huizong), Discussion of Internal Energy in Taijiquan and Traditional Medical Theory" (Taijiquan Nei Qi Qiantan yu Jingluo Xueshuo). The first volume of the Compendium has already been published in Japanese in Japan. In 1988, a Beijing publishing house, Gaodeng Jiaoyu Chubanshe, released a teaching videotape, "Transmission of Art of Chenstyle Taijiquan", that features Chen Zhenglei performing Taijiquan and explaining its origin, contents and practical applications.

In response to numerous invitations from Japan, France, Italy, Switzerland, Hongkong, and the United States, Master Chen has gone abroad numerous times to teach Taijiquan. In China alone, he has taught thousands of visitors from more than 15 different countries and regions. Over 20 Chenstyle Taijiquan Associations and Research Societies have been established overseas. Master Chen Zhenglei's students have gone on to matriculate at the Beijing and Wuhan Physical Education Institutes and he has trained over 15 of the coaches at those prestigious institutions. He has served as the Principal of Chenjiagou Taijiquan School (appointed 1987), established the Chenjiagou Taijiquan Promotion Center (1987) and served as its Head Coach, as Vice Director and Head Coach of Pingdingshan Martial Arts Research Institute (1988), and as a Secretary and Standing Member of the Governing Committee of Henan Province (1985) and National Taijiquan Associations. In 1985, during a visit to Japan as a member of a high-level Chenstyle delegation, he performed for the Emperor of Japan and was invited to the Imperial Palace as a guest. Master Chen also serves as Taijiquan Advisor, Honorary Head and Chairman of Japanese, American (San Franciso, 1990), French, and Italian Chenstyle Taijiquan organizations.

In 1986, he was appointed to be a standing member of Jiaozuo City Political Advisory Committee, and was selected as a Representative to the Henan Province People's Congress in 1988. In 1991, Master Chen was chosen by the editorial department of the China Biographical Yearbook to be listed in the 1991 edition. In 1992, he was selected as a National Level High Grade Martial Arts Coach. In 1993, Wenxian Chenstyle Taijiquan Research Association was established and Master Chen was selected as its head. In 1993, he was also invited by the Japanese "Chenstyle Taijiquan Study Association" to be its advisor. In May of 1993, he went to French Polynesia to teach Taijiquan at the invitation of interested persons there. In July of the same year he went to Malaysia to teach. In December 1993, a written piece of his was selected for publication in Outstanding Individuals of Contemporary reform.

Master Chen visited the United States in August 1996 to teach at the 1996 United States Wushu Association's Special Seminar and International Taijiquan Championship. In April 1999, he and his student Mr. Zhang Xinhu visited and taught Taijiquan in Italy, in late April of the same year he he went to teach Taijiquan in England; in 2000, he published video works of Old Frame Routines Ⅰ & Ⅱ of Chen Style Taijiquan, Single Sword Routine, Pushhand, New Frame Routine I of Chen Style Taijiquan, Health Preservation Taiji; in February 2002, he published books of《Chenshi Taiji Quan, Jian, Dao》,《Taiji Shenyun》; in March 2002, he went to France and taught Taijiquan there; in April, May 2002, he and Mr. Zhang Xinhu taught Taijiquan in Italy again.

陈正雷大师简介

陈正雷大师,1949 年 5 月生于太极拳发祥地——中国河南温县陈家沟,陈氏十九世,太极拳第十一代嫡宗传人,温县陈氏太极拳研究会会长,中国陈家沟太极拳推广中心总教练。现任河南省武术协会副主席,国家武术高级教练,国家级社会体育指导员,中国武术协会委员,中国体育科学学会委员,中国当代“十大武术名师”。

陈正雷大师自八岁起,跟随著名太极拳大师、伯父陈照丕(原南京中央国术馆名誉教授、国术国考评委、64 年被选为全国武协委员)练习家传太极拳术、刀、枪、剑、杆等器械及推手,并孜孜不倦地体验和钻研太极运动的原理及系统理论,直至 1972 年伯父病故。之后,又随太极拳大师,堂叔父陈照奎继续深造,专习叔祖陈发科传授下来的太极拳术、推手技巧以及拳论。

陈正雷大师受两位宗师言传身教二十余载，把继承家传技艺、发扬光大太极文化做为自己终生的奋斗目标，所以，能屡屡战胜各种艰难与困苦，矢志不移地勤学苦练，持之以恒，使自己的功夫深厚纯正，理论水平达到了一个新高度。有“太极金刚”之美称，享誉国内外。

1974 年至 1987 年连续十多次获省武运会、太极拳、剑、推手比赛优秀奖、金牌，蝉联两届全国太极拳大赛冠军。参加并获得两届全国武术比赛特邀表演奖及观摩交流“金狮奖”等。

1989 年至 1997 年，他所培养的学生，在省及全国武术比赛中共获金牌 65 枚。

1972 年开始传拳授艺，学生遍及全世界各地逾万人次，1996 年 12 月在陈家沟举行收徒仪式，国内在册学生 78 人，1981 年开始接待来访学习太极拳的外宾团体，至今已逾百批。1983 年开始应邀数十次出访日、美、法、意、英等二十余个国家讲学传拳。并被五十余个武术团体聘为太极拳顾问、名誉主席和名誉会长。台湾武术界赠锦旗誉其拳艺“登峰造极”，马来西亚太极拳界赠银盘称他为“太极泰斗”，在国内外武术界享有盛誉。

在练功授拳之余，陈正雷大师致力于挖掘整理太极文化瑰宝，默默笔耕，于 1984 年开始步入理论研究与写作的领域，主要著作有《十段功法论》、《陈氏太极拳械汇宗》、《陈氏太极拳养生功》、《陈氏太极拳术》等，是学习研究太极拳的珍贵资料。部分著作被译成日、英、法、西班牙等国文字，在世界许多国家发行。1988 年高等教育出版社录制由陈正雷大师讲解示范的《世传陈氏太极拳术》教学片，1996 年人民体育出版社录制由陈正雷大师讲授的陈氏太极拳、剑、推手、养生功等系列教学片，并被译成日、英、韩等外文，发行世界各地，2000 年又录制了陈氏太极拳老架一路、二路、单剑、推手、拳械欣赏修订版和陈氏太极拳新架一路、养生功教学片，由人民体育出版社和黄河音像出版社出版，河南陈正雷太极文化有限公司总经销，致力于传播太极文化，造福人类。

随着陈正雷先生对"太极武术事业"的推进和提高，他本人也受到更多人的拥戴、国家的支持和社会的承认：1986 年他被选为焦作市政协常委，1988 年被选为河南省人大代表。曾任陈家沟太极拳学校校长，平顶山太极少林武术研习院院长，1992 年被编入《中国人物年鉴》，1994 年被评为国际太极拳大师，1995 年 12 月被中国武术协会评为中国当代"十大武术名师"，并曾被列入《中国当代教育名人辞典》、《中国当代武术家名典》、《中国民间武术家名典》、《当代改革英才》、《当代技术人才荟萃》和《世界名人录》等权威辞书。

联系电话：0371-6338680　6336676
传真：0371-6338680
联系地址：河南省郑州市商城东路 138 号
网址：http://www.chenzhenglei-ti.com.cn
E-mail：tjsports@chenzhenglei-tj.com.cn

About the Translator

Xu Hailiang, born in Jilin Province of China, in March 1967. He graduated from Henan Pingdingshan City Taiji and Shaolin Wushu Academy and the Wushu Department of Wuhan Physical Culture Institute. He has won numerious championships on Taijiquan, Taiji Swordplay and Shaolin Boxing at national and provincial level for 8 times. At present, he is the coach of Wushu in "Guangdong Province Wushu and Ballroom-dancing College".

He is the initiator of "Good Wushu Translation Studio", the main translator of *THE CHINESE WUSHU EXHIBITION SERIES*. What's more, he has translated over 20 pieces of Chinese Wushu Series VCD and several books about Wushu.

译者简介

徐海亮,1967 年 3 月出生于中国吉林,毕业于河南平顶山市太极少林武术院、武汉体育学院武术系,曾九次荣获国家和省级武术比赛的太极拳、太极剑和少林拳冠军。现任广东省武术体育舞蹈学校武术教练。

他是"好武术翻译工作室"创办人,"中华武术展现工程"主译,现已翻译完成中华武术系列 VCD 光碟二十余部,各类武术书籍多部。

图书在版编目(CIP)数据

陈氏太极拳养生功/陈正雷主编；徐海亮英译.
郑州:中州古籍出版社,2002.10
ISBN 7-5348-2181-9/G·449

Ⅰ.陈… Ⅱ.①陈…②徐… Ⅲ.太极拳,陈氏—套路(武术)—英、汉 Ⅳ.G852.111.9

中国版本图书馆 CIP 数据核字(2002)第 078900 号

The Chen-Style Taijiquan For Life Enhancement

陈氏太极拳养生功

作　者:陈正雷
译　者:徐海亮

责任编辑:张　斌
特邀编辑:刘　欣
出 版 社:中州古籍出版社
（地址:郑州市经五路 66 号　邮政编码:450002）
发行单位:新华书店
承印单位:河南第一新华印刷厂
开本:850mm×1168mm　1/32
印张:5.75　插页:4
字数:146 千字　印数:3 000 册
版次:2002 年 9 月第 1 版　印次:2002 年 10 月第 1 次印刷

书号:ISBN 7-5348-2181-9/G·449　定价:19.00 元
本书如有印装质量问题,由承印厂负责调换

CW01559191

THE VINTAGE DOG SCRAPBOOK

- THE WIRE HAIRED FOX TERRIER -

British Library Cataloguing-in-Publication Data
A catalogue record for this book is available from the British Library

VDB

www.vintagedogbooks.com

THE WIRE FOX TERRIER　　　　Bowes Buxom

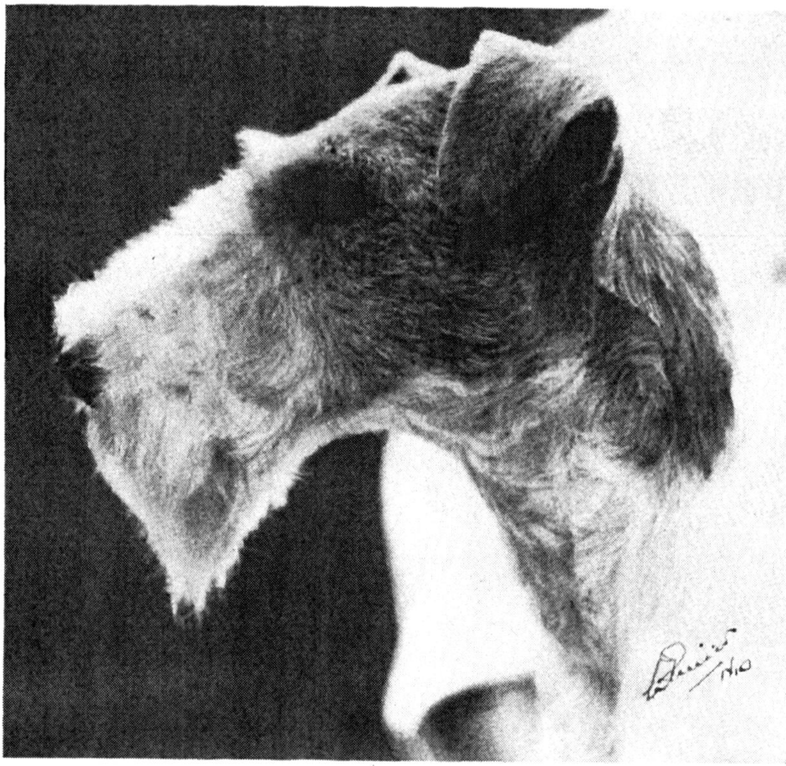

THE WIRE FOX TERRIER — Bowes Buxom

MY DOG

Here is a friend who proves his worth
Without conceit or pride of birth.
Let want or plenty play the host,
He gets the least and gives the most –
He's just a dog.

He's ever faithful, kind and true;
He never questions what I do,
And whether I may go or stay,
He's always ready to obey
'Cause he's a dog

Such meagre fare his want supplies!
A hand caress, and from his eyes
There beams more love than mortals know;
Meanwhile he wags his tail to show
That he's my dog.

He watches me all through the day,
And nothing coaxes him away;
And through the night-long slumber deep
He guards the home wherein I sleep –
And he's a dog.

I wonder if I'd be content
To follow where my master went,
And where he rode – as needs he must –
Would I run after in his dust
Like other dogs.

How strange if things were quite reversed –
The man debased, the dog put first.
I often wonder how t'would be
Were he the master 'stead of me –
And I the dog.

A world of deep devotion lies
Behind the windows of his eyes;
Yet love is only half his charm-
He'd die to shield my life from harm.
Yet he's a dog.

If dogs were fashioned out of men
What breed of dog would I have been?
And would I e'er deserve caress,
Or be extolled for faithfulness
Like my dog here?

As mortals go, how few possess
Of courage, trust, and faithfulness
Enough from which to undertake,
Without some borrowed traits, to make
A decent dog!

- JOSEPH M. ANDERSON

DON'T CALL A MAN A DOG

WHEN we consider how loyal the dog is, even to an evil, cruel master . . . .
WHEN we consider how patient the dog is in this hurly-burly world of ours . . . .
WHEN we consider how the dog possesses the cardinal virtue we humans lack most-to forgive fully. . . .
WHEN we consider how the dog enters wholeheartedly into whatever task is assigned him, unpleasant though it may be . . . .
WHEN we consider that man is the most selfish, designing creature on earth and his dog the most unselfish living thing in the world, risking even life without hesitation . . . .
WHEN we consider how the dog lives a wholesome philosophy of enjoying every passing moment, finding daily delight in living, and to his dying day, retaining a heart of youth . . . .
WHEN we consider how, in the home, the dog by practice and self-example, is a teacher to children and grownups of such qualities as responsibility, obedience, kindness and social altruism . . . .
WHEN we consider all these things and that the dog is the nearest approach on earth to the actual living of the teachings of Jesus of Nazareth . . . .
WHEN we consider all these things – DON'T CALL A MAN A DOG – IT'S UNFAIR TO THE DOG.

THE WIRE FOX TERRIER — "Bowes" Puppies

"FOR RICHER, FOR POORER"

I had a mansion fine; for once
Men said I "rolled in riches;"
Grand paintings hung around its walls,
And statues filled its niches.

The horses in my stable large
Were sleek, well fed, and glossy;
And chief among my dogs I loved
A silken pet, named Flossy.

He dined off fish and fowl and flesh;
By Dukes and Lords was patted;
His wavy coat was daily combed,
And never once seen matted.

He slept on downy satin couch
Within my chamber nightly;
And walked with me o'er velvet lawns,
Whene'er the sun shone brightly.

But ah! there came to me one day
A change most unexpected,-
My wealth took flight, and I was poor,
And homeless, and dejected!

My friends – if *friends* they might be called –
They left me altogether;
Just as the swallows fly away
At chill of wintry weather.

And turning to my dog, I said,
"I leave this house tomorrow;
Will *you* desert me, like the rest,
Or come and share my sorrow?"

The faithful creature licked my hand,
With full eyes overflowing,
That seemed to say, "Your lot is mine;
I go where *you* are going."

We left the place, my dog and I, -
The park-gates closed behind us;
The servants all too busy seemed
To say farewell, or mind us.

We took a cottage, snug and small,
Outside a distant village,
And furnished it too humbly far
For thief to plan its pillage.

I till my own trim garden now.
My dog is ever near me;
He races round the little lawn,
And does his best to cheer me.

I cannot say that *now* he feasts
On food in wasteful measure;
He eats his biscuit hard, and hides
Dry bones as men hide treasure.

And though his coat is never combed,
And looks not fine and glossy,
A dog more full of life and joy
'Twere hard to find than Flossy.

Beside my humble bed at night
He drags a woolly mat in,
And seems to sleep as soundly there
As on a couch of satin.

And oft I say, "My dog! I feel
As if with man disgusted;
The *you*, of all my seeming friends,
Were *only* to be trusted."

- MRS. SURR

COURAGE AND COWARDICE

The wind was rough, the wild waves broke
In thunder on the shore,
As swift a frightened cur rushed by,
Half scared at Ocean's roar.

Through furtive glances at the sea
His eyes their white revealed;
With tail between his legs he ran,
As though his doom were sealed!

Scared from our ears had died away
The lean cur's piteous whine,
When forth a grand retriever sprang
In haste to breast the brine.

A splendid plunge he made for stick,
Flung far in surging tide;
And battling with the crested waves,
Brought back his prize with pride.

O cowardice, we thought, how mean
In man or beast thou art!
But noble courage claims the praise
Of every youthful heart.

No child, however young and small,
But may a hero be;
Hard battles he may fight and win
Upon his bended knee.

For prayer will chase a thousand foes-
Bad tempers, malice, pride;
And, in the strength of God, the hosts
Of hell may be defied.

And soon the happy time shall come
When fighting shall be o'er,
And all the joyful conquerors crowned
Upon the heavenly shore.

- MRS. SURR

THE WIRE FOX TERRIER LANYOR LIGURE

My Dog is Dead

There lies his ball; I wait to see him pounce
And shake it in mock fight which pleases him.
I thought I heard his quick light step again
In playful trot on stairway up and down.

The leash hangs on the wall; I'll shake it loud,
Then joyfully he'll bound into the room
Impatient for his romp. He does not come-
No wistful face peers through half-open door.

The rugs lie smooth; the curtains are not torn.
I haven't missed a shoe or rag today.
The house is dreadfully still, until I wish
I heard four feet come pitpat down the hall.

The soft moist nose that pushed against my hand
The paw that touched me to demand its wish,
The pleading lively eye, the plaintive bark-
What sweet annoyances they now would seem!

The door is open and the gate ajar;
No need to close them-he will not run out.
The new ball throw away; I bought it for
His next birthday-but he will never know.

The Old Dog

The old dog sleeps before the fire
Content to doze the hours away.
His step now drags uncertainly
Where once he frisked 'mid bark and play

Long lies he in the warming sun-
The hunter home from faroff hills,
To run his last and losing race
As eyes grow dim and legs give way.

Keen life still clings within his frame
Yet 'tis but trace of other days
As memory's musings run the chase
In years when legs were swift and strong.

He's deep asleep while muffled bark,
The twitching nose and treading feet
Waft him in dreams across the fields
On trails of game and new-found scent.

Tonight you softly pat his head
As blinking eyes are quick to close.
You miss his wonted nudge and park
When morning finds him still asleep.

You call-he does not open eye
Or wag that ever cheerful tail;
You think him merely sleeping sound-
And soon to leap up joyfully.

Alas, the stiff and stretched out legs,
The breathless loin, the glassy eye
Which oft so soft and moist did plead,
Tell now that death has found its mark!

The brave, stout heart beats now no more
To warm the body whose sole thot
Knew only your command as law-
A servant for your ev'ry wish.

A noble soul has fled the earth,
Which never knew deceit nor guile;
Of man was part, a better part,
Without his treach'rous smile and face.

High up at heaven's gate he waits
Without complaint though long the hours-
An ear pricked up, half-opened eye
To catch quick sight when master comes.

At last a loved familiar face
The watchful dog discerns with joy.
"What sound is that?" the master asks
In strange surprise. No need to wait-

The answer comes in leap and bark-
Old dog, old master once again
Unite to never part as both
In gladsome pace wend way to God.

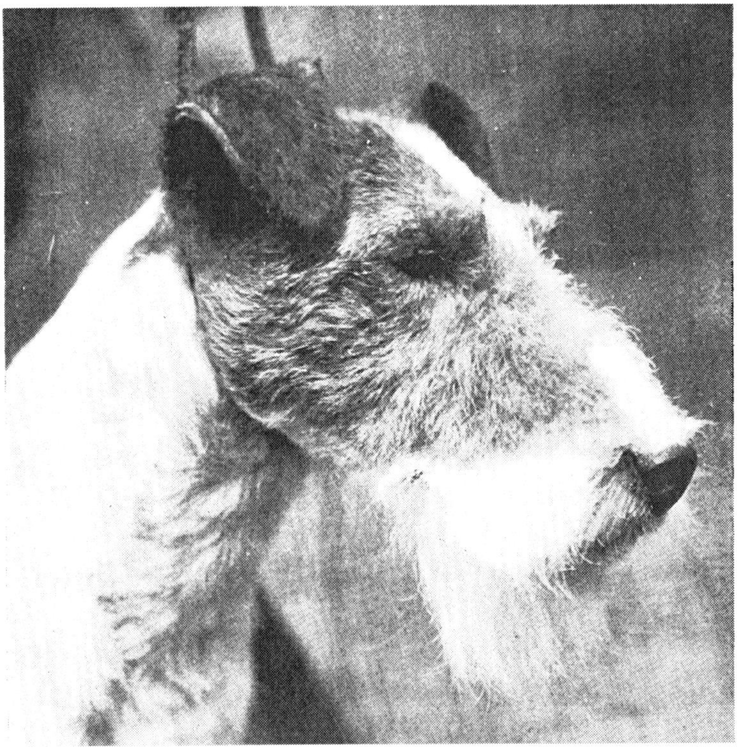

THE WIRE FOX TERRIER — CH. CRACKLEY STARTLER

Dogs, Too, Get Spring Fever

In all lands the return of warming sunshine brings the pleasing spring fever. Dogs too are its willing victims. They find increasing delight in their daily vagabonding. The plain, soft earth after a winter of concealment under the snow, presents myriads of new smells; and as anyone initiated into the inner cult of dog lore can tell you, the hors d'oeuvres of a canine menu are the multitude of smells awaiting detection by the dog's nose in every spot and space.

The paws of the dog itch to be soothed by digging in the once-again soft ground of springtime. A neighbour's lawn has just been dedicated with the planting of flower seeds and shrubbery after a winter of ecstatic reading of the alluring seed catalogues by the hopeful neighbour.

Beware-you will incur your good neighbour's enmity! Act before it is too late! Be certain that your dog harkens to your voice, else you will need to retrieve him in the front yard next door happily scratching up the earth and grass with all fours and looking at you with a devil-may-car, "haven't we got fun?" expression.

It's his forgivable way of expressing spring fever. But-call him quickly and hide yourself away before your neighbour's wife spots you out of the front window. Walk nonchalantly as if you never owned a dog in your life.

And have your wife send to your neighbour's wife that evening as a peace offering, some delicacy she has just cooked, for dogs will be dogs, especially in springtime.

The Dog's Bill of Rights

I. I want nutritious food once daily-not too much; and don't believe the old idea that bones are good for me.

II. I want clean water in a clean dish twice daily.

III. I want a dry, ventilated but draftless place for sleeping.

IV. I want a collar that doesn't choke me or isn't so loose it catches on my head.

V. I want a quiet place in the basement on the Fourth of July

VI. I want every boy reprimanded but softly, who throws stones at me or twists my ears.

VII. I want folks to judge me as a dog and from a dog's viewpoints.

VIII. I want everybody to keep in mind that I do with my mouth, most things they do with their hands; so, they needn't be afraid of a dog's teeth.

IX. I want to be treated sympathetically, just as I treat small children and all those in distress, who belong to my master's clan.

X. I want my mind and body trained so that I can be of the fullest service.

XI. I want to be considered one of the family, for I will give my life to protect it.

XII. I want my master to be my god on earth and to act the part.

SIGNED: for all dogs:

FIDO

THE WIRE FOX TERRIER — CH. LANARTH BRACKEN

Seventeen Training Don'ts

Sometimes what should be done can be said best by telling what should not be done. The reasons for the don'ts should be evident to every person in process of training his dog. Each one is based upon the basic psychology of the dog's mind.

1. Don't punish your dog while you are angry or lack control of yourself.
2. Don't punish your dog with the lead or any instrument of training or anything he should associate with duty or pleasure.
3. Don't sneak up on your dog, grab him from the rear, surprise him or reach for him quickly.
4. Don't chase your dog to catch him; he must come to you or follow after you.
5. Don't coax your dog to you and then turn upon him with punishment. You will regret the deception.
6. Don't trick, fool or taunt your dog. It is cruel and inconsistent to tease your dog to come to you when he can not.
7. Don't punish a dog by stepping on his paws needlessly. They are exceedingly sensitive. Don't twist his ears playfully or otherwise. Don't strike him on the backbone, in the face or on the ears.
8. Don't nag your dog; don't be giving orders to him constantly; don't pester him with your shoutings.

9. Don't praise a dog for doing a certain act, then at a later time scold him for doing the same act. Consistency on your part is a chief virtue in dog training.
10. Don't train your dog within an hour after he has eaten.
11. Don't ever lose patience with a puppy younger than six months and seldom with a dog older.
12. Don't throw or kick a puppy nor lift him by the head or leg or skin of the neck.
13. Don't work your dog without some short rest or play periods during training lesson. A five-minute rest for every twenty minutes of training is desirable. Feats requiring strength and endurance are for a dog older than six months.
14. Don't permit everyone and anyone to give commands to your dog. While you are training him, he must be a one-man dog, depending on you to feed him and care for him.
15. Don't consider tricks the chief purpose in training. Usefulness is the object sought in all instruction of the dog. Acts that spring naturally from the dog's instincts are to be fostered.
16. Don't expect your dog to be a wonderful dog after a few weeks of training; four months to a year may be necessary in order to make the master proud of him, but the work is worth the effort. Training never ends.
17. Don't jump to the conclusion that your dog is dumb. He may differ with you, believing the trainer should know more than the dog.

30 DON'TS FOR EVERY DOG OWNER

Don't surprise a sleeping dog nor approach any dog without giving him notice.
Don't make a sissy of your dog by coddling him.
Don't allow the dog to become chilled after bathing.
Don't give worm medicine to a sick dog.
Don't exercise the dog within thirty minutes after he has eaten.
Don't allow strangers to chastise the dog.
Don't fear a dog merely because he is frothing at the mouth.
Don't allow the dog to lie constantly near the radiator in winter.
Don't fondle or pet strange dogs.
Don't give quantities of water to a dog that is vomiting.
Don't allow dogs to sit in any and all chairs in the home.
Don't take dogs needlessly into strange kennels as there is danger of disease.
Don't allow the dog to roam by himself; he should always be within sight of his master.
Don't beat a dog; a light stroke with a few loosely rolled sheets of newspaper plus shaming with the voice generally are sufficient.
Don't believe that eating of meat by the dog will make it "go mad."
Don't give castor oil for all forms of constipation.
Don't neglect paying (and promptly too) for damages your dog may have done.
Don't pour kerosene on a dog's skin for killing fleas.
Don't neglect calling a veterinarian promptly for your sick dog since both dog and doctor want to live.

Don't encourage needless dog fights.
Don't attempt to take a bone away from a dog without first calling his attention to yourself; never interfere with a strange dog while it is eating.
Don't feed any very small or sharp-pointed bones.
Don't let your dog sleep in a draft or in a damp place.
Don't let everybody pet your dog if he is to be a watchdog.
Don't shout commands to your dog in an excited tone of voice.
Don't kill your dog by overfeeding him.
Don't run the risk of losing your dog by not having your name and address on his collar plate.
Don't try to avoid paying a dog license fee.
Don't let your dog cross the street without being by your side, even if well trained, or on lead.
Don't believe everything poorly informed people tell you about dogs.

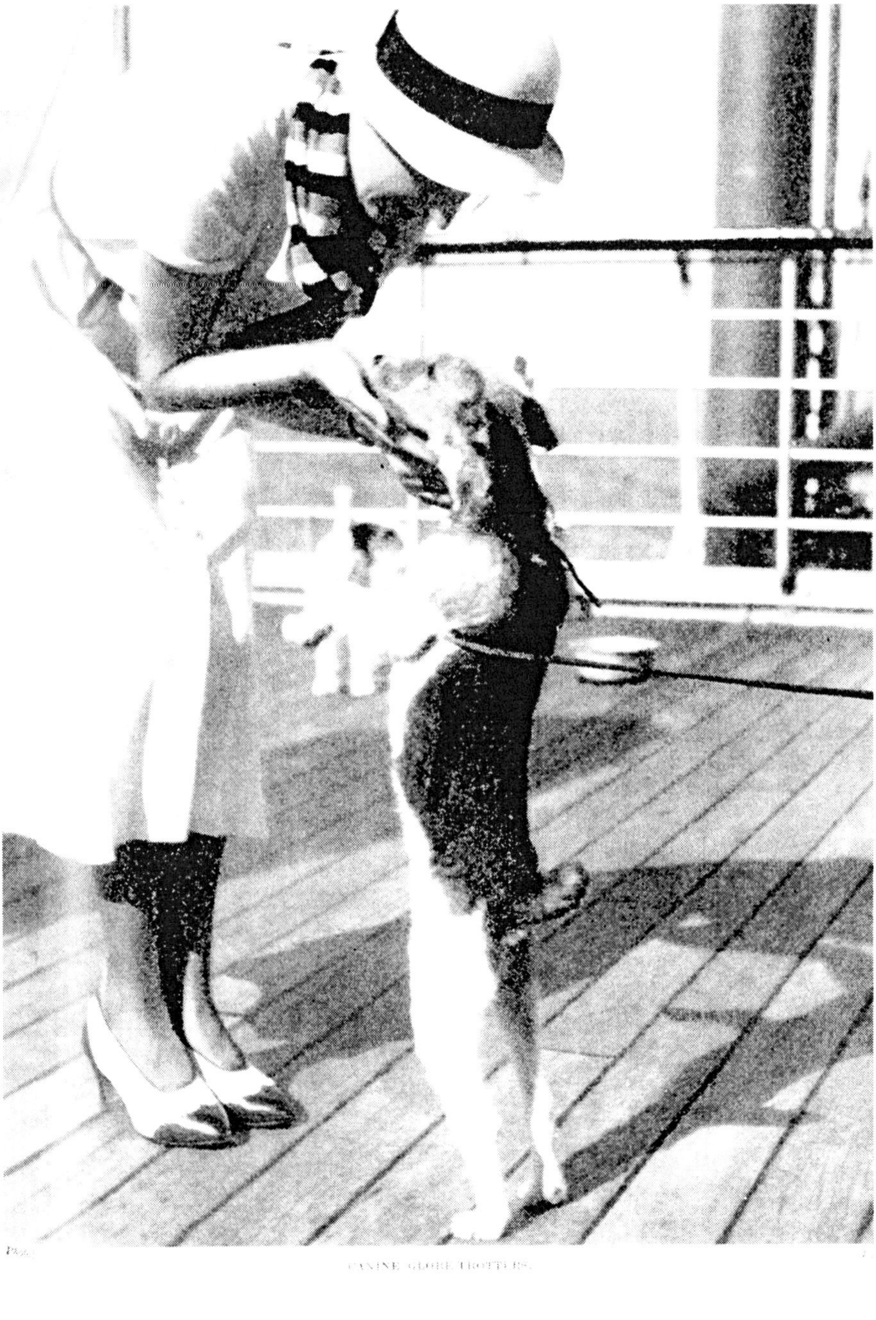

CANINE GLOBE-TROTTERS.

A Dozen Dog Care Do's

1. Trim toenails every three months with heavy scissors or regular nail trimmer.
2. Have a set day each month for examining your dog externally inch by inch, including "smelling the ears."
3. Brush or wipe the teeth and gums with a soft cloth weekly and weakly, either dry or slightly soaked in salt-and soda water solution.
4. Watch the frequency, colour and consistency of bowel movements as symptom of ailing condition.
5. Feed your dog each day at the same scheduled hour and spot, and in the same food pan.
6. Brush your dog with a not-too-soft brush vigorously every day, no matter how lazy you yourself feel.
7. Take your dog and yourself out for three romps a day, one of which should be extra long.
8. Keep our dog, no matter how well trained, on a lead and close to you, (on your left) when on busy streets and in crowds.
9. Sun and air the dog's bedding once a week.
10. Cure a skin disease at first notice and before it has a chance to intensify.
11. Prolong your dog's life by keeping him away from the dinner table at mealtime and from eating frequently.
12. Have patience with your dog just as he 'puts up' with you. Be sympathetic with his limitations.

The Dog Gives Training Advice to His Master

Now, look here, human; I realize you've got to know more than the dog before you can teach him, but please mix common sense and good judgment with your knowledge.

I can't talk with words. You can teach me to lie down with the command UP. The big job you have in this training work with me as your pupil is to get your ideas across to me. Don't worry about my end of it, if I can figure out in my dog mind what you want me to do.

And incidentally, nine times of ten a dog disobeys, he isn't actually dong that-he just doesn't get what you had in mind. Believe me, we dogs have only one big act on our program-to win your approval in everything we do. I know it's misplaced devotion at times but we'll skip that.

Just remember, master, that we are dogs-and glad of it too. We aren't humans and don't want to be. To us this is a dog's world, mostly of smells and sounds. We don't want to be called humans-that's unfair to us.

But when you map out a training course look at it from the dog's viewpoint. Does the act appeal to our love of play, our desire to please our interest in getting something to eat, our curiosity in seeing what's happening on the other side of the fence> Put a canine angle on your training efforts-and we'll respond. We want to be all dog, and not half human.

Do you recall the famous court case in which Sam Smith was tried for shooting a dog that leaped over his fence, dug up his garden, and bit one of the Smith children badly? Well, the jury convicted Smith but we dogs took a vote and decided that the dog's owner should have been found guilty instead.

When one of us is taken to the pound in the dog catcher's truck and there murdered legally if no one reclaims us, our blood is no the soul of the owner who thought so little of us that he did not keep us under his control.

And why shouldn't we in turn set forth the essential qualities of a successful trainer? We want our trainers to possess an abundance of FOUR things:

1. Patience with its twin, self-control.
2. Seriousness of purpose, for the trainer is moulding our characters; and this seriousness demands that he concentrate on his training work similarly as he requires us.
3. Consistency of methods and aims, so that we will not be confused or deceived.
4. Sincere love for us dogs.

I might bark in passing that we laugh in our paw when you humans, our assumed gods, lose your temper over us, shout commands excitedly, are inconsistent in not sticking to the same command for the same obedience or let us get away with pretended deafness when you speak to us.

At any rate, just look at things through our eyes and minds; make yourself one of us for the time being when you are training us-you don't really train us-we can do all this sort of stuff naturally; you're just kind of dumb in getting it out of use.

Signed - - for all dogs, FIDO

Photo [Topical

FULL OF FUN.

Wire-hair Terriers in general, and puppies of that breed in particular, have a great sense of fun. They are always on the look-out for a game or a frolic The five shown above are from the O'Groats Kennels, Saltford, near Bristol.

A DOG'S TRAGEDY

On his morning rounds the Master
Goes to learn how all things fare;
Searches pasture after pasture,
Sheep and cattle eyes with care;
And, for silence or for talk,
He hath comrades in his walk;
Four dogs, each pair of different breed,
Distinguished two for scent, and two for speed.

See a hare before him started!
-Off they fly in earnest chase;
Every dog is eager-hearted,
All the four are in the race:
And the hare whom they pursue
Knows from instinct what to do;
Her hope is near: no turn she makes;
But, like an arrow, to the river takes.

Deep the river was, and crusted
Thinly by a one night's frost;
But the nimble hare hath trusted
To the ice, and safely crost;
She hath crost, and without heed
All are following at full speed,
When, lo! the ice, so thinly spread,
Breaks – and the greyhound, Dart, is over head!

Better fate have Prince and Swallow –
See them cleaving to the sport!
Music has no heart to follow,
Little Music, she stops short,
She hath neither wish nor heart,

Hers is now another part:
A loving creature she, and brave"
And fondly strives her struggling friend to save.

From the brink her paws she stretches,
Very hands as you would say!
And afflicting moans she fetches,
As he breaks the ice away.
For herself she hath no fears,-
Him alone she sees and hears,-
Makes efforts with complainings; nor gives o'er
Until her fellow sinks to reappear no more.

- WORDSWORTH

DOG LATIN

Eheu! hie jacet Crony,
A dog of much renown,
Nee fur, nee macaroni,
Though born and bred in town.

In war he was acerrimus,
In dog-like arts perite,
In love, alas! miserrimus,
For he died of a rival's bite.

His mistress struxit cenotaph;
And, as the verse comes pat in,
Ego qui scribo epitaph
Indite it in dog Latin.

- UNKNOWN

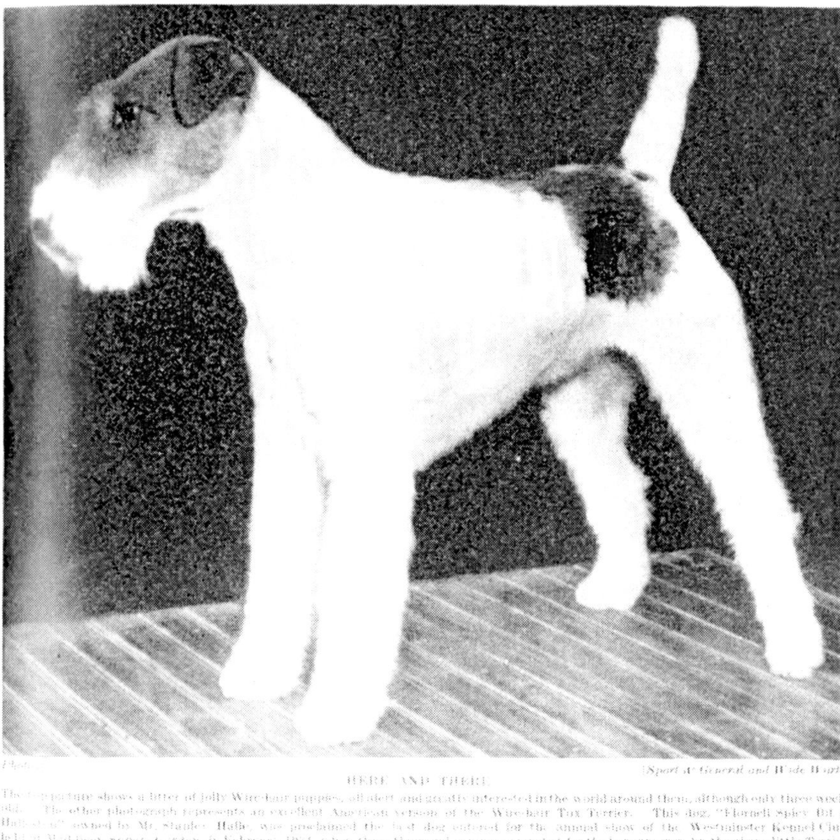

Photos   [*Sport & General and Wide World.*

HERE AND THERE

The top picture shows a litter of jolly Wire-hair puppies, all alert and greatly interested in the world around them, although only three weeks old. The other photograph represents an excellent American version of the Wire-hair Fox Terrier. This dog, "Flornell Spicy Bit of Halleston" owned by Mr. Stanley Halle, was proclaimed the best dog entered for the annual show of the Westminster Kennel Club, held at Madison Square Gardens in February 1934, when three thousand canines competed for the honours won by the above little Terrier.

Cats versus Dogs

We like cats. They furnish running exercise for dogs and always win the race. They are a living, moving thing of beauty, softness and grace. They and the birds are among the few animals that wash themselves.

Like the dog, they are a heritage from the wilderness. But whereas Fido the dog has made an almost complete adjustment between savagery and civilisation, Pussy the cat clings to most of her ancestors' ways.

She is still a member of her ancient race of tigers, lions and panthers. She is a tiger of small size who deigns to favour you with her presence in your house, sleeping haughtily at your very fireplace. She permits you to occupy the house with her. Her lair demands her loyalty for she prefers it even though the family moves away.

She moves with all the proudness of her proud race. One would think that such diminutive descendant of the lion and the tiger would be marked with humility. Her very whiskers, pure relic of the jungle and its shadows, exude haughtiness. She washes herself publicly that all may see the rite of the elite.

She likes the darkness; her paths are those of the night; the starts evoke the melody of her soul (on these nocturnal romantic occasions, more commonly "his" soul).

She travels along. Who has seen a pack of cats? Secrecy confided to no one, is her abiding trait.

Behind those greenish-yellow gleaming eyes, guarded by pupils now round, no but an upright slit, reside mystery, adventure, and dark plannings.

She possesses a most uncertain disposition. Her set countenance starting at your face shamelessly may mean friendliness or a scratch. That gracefully agile tail may be but a salute to those about to die. She is a daughter of many moods, royal in her fits of temper.

Where the cat is a pet, the dog is a companion. Where the cat is a lady, the dog is a roustabout. Where the cat is disdainful, the dog is a good fellow. Where the cat is unconcerned with its mistress, the dog imitates the moods of his master.

We use "she" when speaking of cats but refer to the dog as "he" and could there be more conclusive proof of what we are trying to argue than this natural choice of pronoun in the third person.

THE FRIEND OF MAN

With eye upraised his master's look to scan,
The joy, the solace, and the aid of man;
The rich man's guardian and the poor man's friend,
The only creature faithful to the end.

UNKNOWN

Photo] [*E.N.A*

EXCLUSIVE.

The former Crown Prince of Germany with his favourite dog, a Fox Terrier. His Royal Highness kindly posed for this photograph for exclusive publication in *Hutchinson's Dog Encyclopaedia*, adding his autograph to the picture reproduced above.

Have a Heart, Mr. Dog Owner

The following written by the author applies to the puppy just purchased, perhaps from a distant kennel, and now arrived in the home of its new owner. Most puppies are purchased "at a distance," and at the tender age of about four months.

NOTHING is more pathetic and at the same time more courageous than a few-months-old puppy literally pulled away from its mother, from its brothers and sisters; then pushed into a crate, shaken upon a jolting journey, finally to be ushered into the presence of strangers in its new home, whose selection certainly has been without its choice or knowledge.

THE SLATS are torn off the crate – a commotion enough to terrify even an old dog. The little breathing bunch of softness is cold, hungry, trembling after the roughness of travel, and with it all, a sickness it never knew before – that of loneliness.

FAR FROM HOME and playmates, and the world it has known, it peers out of the crate with frightened yet trusting eyes.

IT LOOKS ABOUT only to be disappointed for it had fancied dimly in its baby mind, that in some way, at the end of the journey, mother and the rest the family would be there to welcome it with a pretended sniff of curiosity and then would resume the customary play.

THE PAT OF a hand, a saucer of milk, a few softly spoken words, and almost a miracle transpires.

THE TAIL WAGS. The eyes become less drawn; they look up at you with a sort of soulful pleading. The legs wobble a bit, then walk.

THE CRATE, THE trembling and the unfriendly world are forgotten. The pup begins to explore the new home, every crack and corner – and ten days later, owns the house and everything in it, including yourself.

In Praise of the Female

NOTWITHSTANDING that prejudice often prefers her brother, the female dog has all the virtues of her species and fewer of the vices. Indeed it may be said that she excels the male in most of the good qualities which have endeared the dog to us as man's best friend.

IN A DOG we demand companionship, watchful guarding and usefulness as the occasion requires. These the female gives in greater measure and more gracefully than does the male.

HER COMPANIONSHIP is mellowed with a devotion more steadfast and gentle, ever given with the subtle charm of her sex.

SHE IS A keener watcher, feels a more constant sense of duty, and with motherly suspicion, discriminates more carefully between friend of the family and the stranger.

THE HOUSEWIFE has less trouble with conduct, fewer pieces of bric-a-brac to mend, and less sweeping to do.

HER GOOD manners are evident in the finesse with which she eats, in contrast to the male's greedy gulping.

IF HOUSEBREAKING can be regarded as a nasty task, choose the female-she is cleaner in the home, does her duties less frequently, and outdoors surely does them more modestly and over smaller area.

THE FEMALE is a homebody, jealous of the family possessions, whereas her brother may incline to be the tramp. The guilt of digging up a neighbour's flowers usually must be placed upon the roaming male.

THE FEMALE is less presumptuous unless it be with children; in them she assumes a motherly interest. She senses danger more quickly. The extra attention she pays to the baby of the household reveals an instinctive solicitude for the weak and helpless.

TRAINERS PREFER the female for she learns more quickly and keeps her mind on the task at hand. Her conscience is more sensitive to disobedience. On game in the field, she is fully as keen and successful.

WHEREAS THE male is in season all the year, the female comes into heat only twice a year and then for a scarce twenty days; she asks only that she be kept at home or, if outdoors, on a lead, during these brief periods.

IN NOTHING ELSE is the prejudice against the female dog (let us not hesitate to call her openly by the ancient and honourable name of bitch) so evident and unfair as with regard to her heat. When she has matured and in turn is ready to repeat the divine mystery of birth, she is shunned, almost cursed as though her sex were a plague, as though she should be punished for her sex and for the creative duties Nature has decreed for all of her sex in all species of animal life.

IN PUREBRED breeding, the female is just as important (and not a few authorities of heredity declare her more dominant) as the stud male; her pedigree is to be studied just as carefully.

FURTHER SHE has the advantage of motherhood; it is she who carries the allotment of coming life. She can be mated and thereby add her bit to the family's income through presenting her owner with duplicates of herself to carry on in other homes.

LOGICALLY INDEED the female is to be preferred to the male, and the prospective purchaser of a puppy well can place the advantage with her in making his choice.

CAN YOUR DOG DO THIS? [E. Field]

DIFFERENCES IN DOGS

Ay, in the catalogue ye go for men;
As hounds, and greyhounds, mongrels, spaniels, curs,
Shoughs, water-rugs, and demi-wolves are clepped
All by the name of dogs: the valued file
Distinguishes the swift, the slow, the subtle,
The housekeeper, the hunter, every one
According to the gift which bounteous nature
Hath in him closed; whereby he does receive
Particular addition from the bill
That writes them all alike: and so of men.

- SHAKESPEARE

THE DOG IN THE MANGER

An envious Dog that Brooding lay,
Upon a Crop Replete with Hay,
Snarls at the Ox that thither came,
An eager appetite to tame.
And forced him back, incensed, whereat
He on the Dog invokes this Fate:-
May the Just Gods so punish thee,
As thy Rude Spleen hath injured me,
Who Does prohibit me the meat,
Whereon they Self disdains to eat.

- APHRA BEHN (AESOP)

MR. F. REDMOND'S CH. DUSKY CRACKER
BY CH. CACKLER OF NOTTS—DUSKY RUTH.
Photograph by Reveley, Wantage.

Why Own a Dog

THAT you may not forget how to play as exemplified by the dog who carries his puppy heart on through into the graying muzzle.

THAT you may have for your home and possessions an alert burglar alarm and a policeman who never sleeps.

THAT you may be reminded daily and with resultant humility that you and the animal kingdom are of one and the same group in the scheme of creation.

THAT you may live above petty selfishness through obligating yourself for the welfare of one who depends implicitly upon you and never complains if you are derelict.

THAT you may forget the worries of the day and the strain of its routine as arriving home, you are greeted with unfeigned delight by one whose heart is filled only with thought of you and whose existence, he believes, cannot go on apart from yours.

THAT you may find surcease from being bored through observing the dog's freshness in doing the customary little things, his curiosity over the flutter of a leaf to the ground, and his discovery of new delights along old paths.

THAT your children, growing up with a dog, may see a daily living sermon on kindness, obligation to others and the necessity for obedience, and that later they can translate these qualities into good citizenship.

THAT you may learn from your servant the dog to live with faith in fellowmen, with a readiness to forgive, and above all, with an unselfishness which may not be logical but is divinely refreshing.

THAT by your dog's contagious example, you may live each day to its fullness, be always ready for new adventure, and find zest in common and uncommon things alike.

THAT all these things may come to pass.

GET A DOG

OWN A DOG

AND BE OWNED BY A DOG.

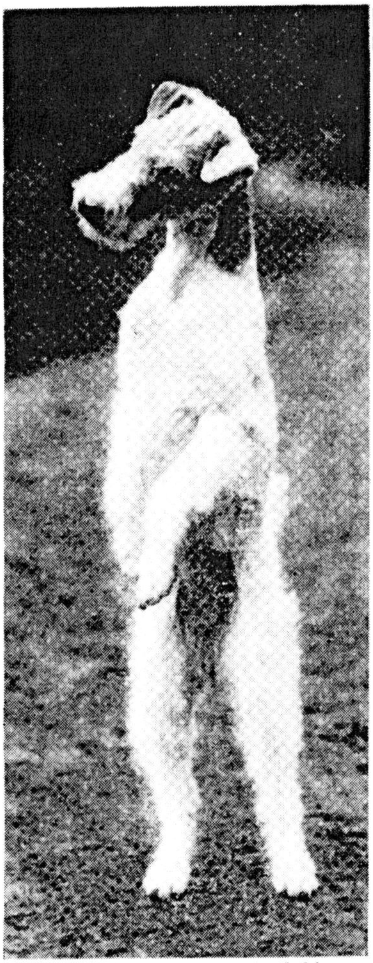

Photo] [*R. Robinson.*

CLEVER.

"Wires" are very intelligent and will learn all sorts of tricks.

Breeder's Code

1. I will study the bitch as well as the sire.
2. I will study grandparents rather than parents.
3. I will not pay attention to breeding superstitions.
4. I will interpret a pedigree by breeding facts and dominance rather than names and titles.
5. I will keep full breeding records and draw conclusions accordingly.
6. I will put away culls, weaklings and the deformed shortly after birth.
7. I will not breed, sell or give away a shy or excessively nervous dog.
8. I will judge a stud by his offspring even to the third generation.
9. I will honour most the bred-by-exhibitor dog.
10. I will give preference to breeding specimens of good temperament and strong nerves.
11. I will have patience to try again and again, and will not be discouraged by litters which are disappointments.
12. I will be led on constantly by the seductive dream of one day producing the perfect dog of my breed, and if another breeder forges ahead of me, I shall envy but also praise him.

The Dogist's Code

(Note – Henry L. Mencken in his Dictionary of American Language Vol. II., credits the author Will Judy with the origin of the word dogist.)

I. Colour all your work with a deep love for all dogs.

II. Be sympathetic counsellor to the novice for you yourself once knew as little as he.

III. Beware of him who is quick to find fault for likely you will be his target in time.

IV. Say nothing rather than out of malice, speak ill of another kennel or breed.

V. Seek business on your own merit rather than by taking it away from a competitor.

VI. Envy the competitor who forges ahead of you, but praise him also.

VII. Win with a smile of course, but to lose with a smile lessens the defeat and requires greater sportsmanship.

VIII. When you lose, resolve to come back to win at a later time.

IX. Show in yourself the same sportsmanship you demand of others.

X. Be the god-on-earth and all-wise master your dogs think you are.

MR. J. J. HOLGATE'S CH. SOUTHBORO' SALEX
BY CH. SYLVAN RESULT—MARCHARD CORONA.

THE DOG AND THE SHADOW

The Dog who with his prey the River swam
Saw his own laden Image in the stream.
The wishing Cur grown covetous of all,
To catch the Shadow lets the Substance fall.
- APHRA BEHN (AESOP)

THE DOGS OF NILE

Like the dogs of Nile be wise;
Who, taught by instinct how to shun
The crocodile, that lucking lies,
Run as they drink, and drink and run.
- SWIFT

WELCOMING THE DAWN

At morning's call
The small-voiced pug-dog welcomes in the sun,
And flea-bit mongrels, wakening one by one,
Give answer all.
- HOLMES

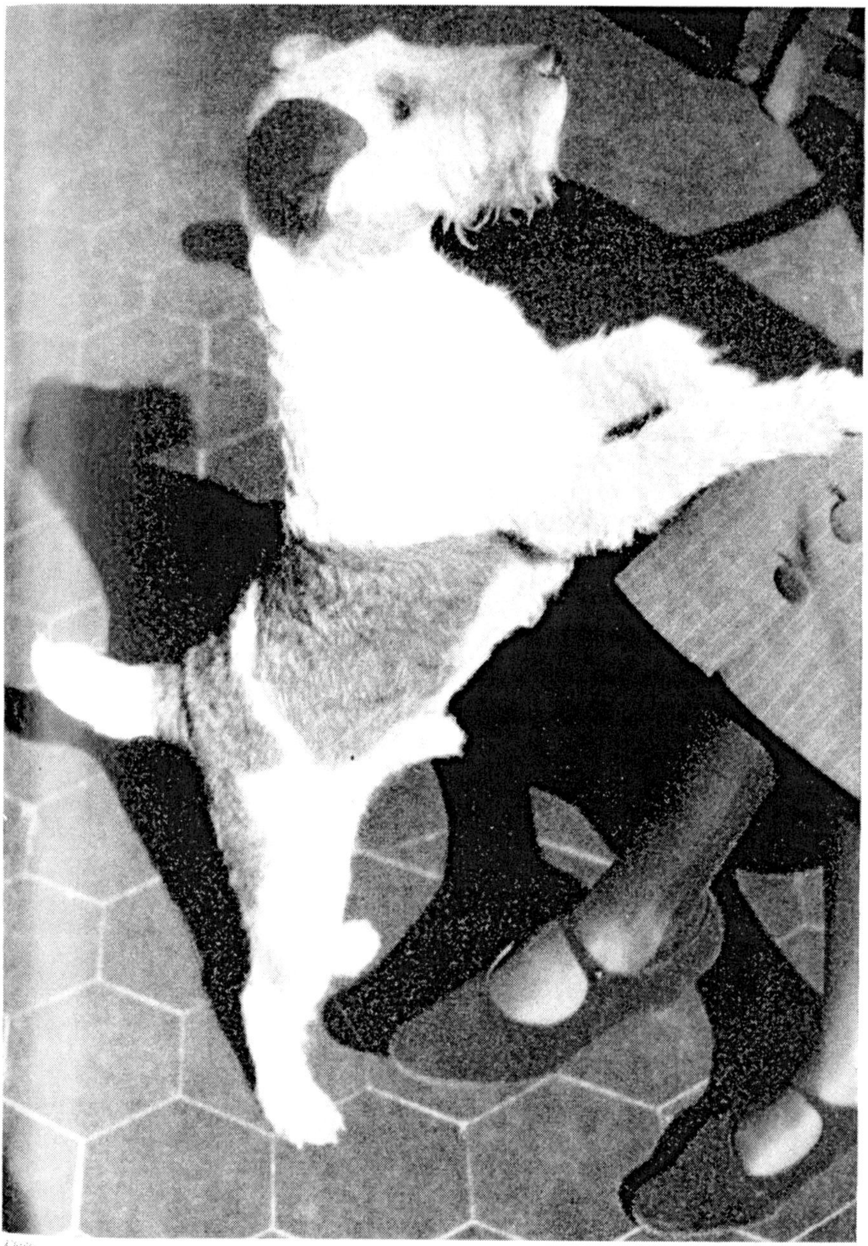

Photo.] [Doreen Leigh.

APPEALING.

If there is such a thing as "eye-appeal", surely the Wire-hair Terrier has got it to the last degree. Judging by its expression this one seems to say "Won't you take me for a walk ?"

The Spirit of Sportsmanship

(A word of counsel to exhibitors at dog shows)

Dog shows are fascinating, thrilling, interesting. The afford opportunity for social contacts, for friendly gatherings, for sportsmen to gather from all sections of America. To win a blue or even the second red in strong competition gives deep pleasure.

The dogs themselves receive the best of care; in truth, most of them enjoy going away from the kennels to be posed in the show ring.

A dog may win against another mostly because he presents his good points to better advantage before the judge; he is "on his toes," properly posed for his particular breed. At tomorrow's show he may lose to the same dog.

If you have what you consider a typy specimen, enter him at one or more dog shows to get an official opinion through a licensed judge.

The placing of your dog at one show is only one man's opinion of your dog-the judge's, and on that particular day, it is official for that show. But the next show, another judge, liking your type of dog, and under different competition, may place your dog first. Few good dogs go through to the title without losing perhaps two of every five times.

One dog show does not make or break a dog. Some great winners were defeated at their first show.

Of course, you have the best dog in the world, until you meet another dog owner, and he will tell you that he has the best dog in the world. Both of you will be mostly right.

"Ten Commandments" for the Dog Owner

I. Give your dog a monthly physical examination: check his skin for possible irritation; "smell" the inside of his ears for possible canker infection. Every six months have his toe nails cut and teeth cleaned.

II. On snowy, rainy, slushy days, have a large, rough, absorbent towel just inside the door, within reach. Use it vigorously to clean, wipe, and dry the dog down to the skin-especially between the toes-when he comes back from his romp outdoors.

III. When you have guests in the house, make certain the dog does not paw the ladies' stockings; does not leap on the guests; does not make a nuisance of himself in any way.

IV. At least every two days, brush the dog's coat thoroughly – brush tenderly around ears and head. Make certain the bristles of the brush reach down to the skin in order to remove dandruff and other impurities.

V. Train your dog so that he knows his place in the house. It is never in the dining room while you are eating; never sleeping against the radiator, nor at top or bottom of stairways, nor in hallways. Have a definite place designated for him where to eat and sleep.

VI. Regard your dog as a dog and not as half-human; no "baby talk," no coddling.

VII. Do not wait until it is too late to take your dog to the veterinarian. Both the dog and the doctor want to live.

VIII. Have regard for your neighbours and their rights and wishes by keeping your dog under control so that he does not damage their lawns or cause them annoyance.

IX. Do not permit your dog to become a public nuisance or cause unsanitary conditions.

X. Do not be unkind to your dog by overfeeding him so that he becomes lazy, unwatchful, clumsy, and ill.

CH. "GRANDON MASTERPIECE".

Born in October 1929, this Terrier was bred by Dr. Fisher, and is owned by Mr. J. Cross, of Warrington. "Masterpiece" is a son of "Crackley Supremacy".

LEGS.—*Viewed from any direction should be*

All photos] [*Hedges.*

CH. "EPPING EDITOR".

This short-bodied, long-headed dog, owned by Mr. A. A. W Simmonds, is a son of Ch. "Talavera Simon".

INT. CH. "BEAU BRUMMEL OF WILDOAKS".

A son of "Signal of Warily of Wildoaks" and the Int. Ch. "Gains Great Surprise of Wildoaks". The latter was bred by Mr. J. C. Pickering, and was born in January, 1926.

CH. "EPPING ELDORADO".

Also one of Mr. A. A. W. Simmonds' noted Terriers. This winner of five Championship Certificates goes back to Ch. "Fountain Crusader".

THE UNDER DOG

I know that the world, the great big world,
Will never a moment stop
To see which dog may be in the fault,
But will shout for the dog on top.
But for me, I shall never pause to ask
Which dog may be in the right,
For my heart will beat, while it beats at all,
For the underdog in the fight.

- ANONYMOUS

BEAU'S REPLY

Sir, when I flew to seize the bird
In spite of your command,
A louder voice than yours I heard,
And harder to withstand.

You cried – forbear – but in my breast
A mightier cried – proceed –
'Twas nature, sir, whose strong behest
Impelled me to the deed.

Yet much as nature I respect,
I ventured once to break
(As you perhaps may recollect)
Her precept for your sake;

And when your linnet on a day,
Passing his prison door,
Had fluttered all his strength away,
And panting pressed the floor,

Well knowing him a sacred thing,
Not destined to my tooth,
I only kissed his ruffled wing,
And licked the feathers smooth.

Let my obedience then excuse
My disobedience now,
Nor some reproot yourself refuse
From your aggrieved Bow-wow:

If killing birds be such a crime
(Which I can hardly see),
What think you, sir, of killing time
With verse addressed to me?

- COWPER

MR. C. HOULKER'S

CH. DUSKY ADMIRAL

BY COMMODORE OF NOTTS—DUSKY RUTH.

A Dog's Prayer for His Master

O LORD OF HUMANS, make my master faithful to his fellowmen as I am to him. Grant that he may be devoted to his friends and family as I am to him.

MAY HE BE openfaced and undeceptive as I am; may he be true to trust reposed in him as I am to his.

GIVE HIM a face cheerful like unto my wagging tail. Give him a spirit of gratitude like unto my licking tongue.

FILL HIM WITH patience like unto mine that awaits his footsteps uncomplainingly for hours. Fill him with my watchfulness, my courage, and my readiness to sacrifice comfort or life itself.

KEEP HIM always young in heart and crowded with the spirit of play, even as I.

MAKE HIM as good a man as I am dog. Make him worthy of me, his dog.

CLEVER DRAWINGS BY VERE TEMPLE, SHOWING THE WIRE-HAIR TERRIER IN VARYING MOODS.

STILL 'MAN'S BEST FRIEND'

Bringing up a puppy to doghood is an achievement and also a practical course in teaching. One becomes a master of animal psychology and an expert in pedagogy. Even the bachelor and spinster dog owners go through the similar duties of a parent.

But the work and the worry, the cleaning up after the puppy, the reprimands and the disappointments – all are worth while and are well repaid by the dog as he develops into an appreciative, loyal, obedient, faithful member of the household.

A little soft warm bundle of fur which came into your home greatly frightened, biologically one of the beasts of the field, has almost bridged the wide gap between the human race and the animal kingdom. He has come out of the fields and forests of his ancestors to live by your side in the midst of modern civilization; and he makes the adjustment splendidly.

There is no other instance of such great progress from one stage to another as that of the dog, which adjusts himself to all the needs and desires of man. He comes from savagery to civilization within the short period of twelve months and indeed represents man's greatest achievement over the animal kingdom.

Give that four-footed member of your family the consideration and care to which you are obligated; and when in old age he moves slowly, his eyes water, and he dreams of puppyhood days, his passing on will be that of a loved and lovable member of the family whose soul never knew dishonesty and deceit.

THE MIRACLE OF MATING AND BIRTH

The work of dog breeding has these progressive steps – choice of parents, the mating, the period of in whelp or pregnancy of the dam or bitch, the whelping of the litter of puppies, nursing and care of puppies for the first eight weeks, care, development and supervision of the poppies after eight weeks.

But the most interesting, most fascinating of the six steps is the delivery or whelping of the puppies out of the mother's womb. Something new comes into the world of conscious being; life appears for the first time to the outside world; the miracle of mating and birth is being climaxed. The spark of being bursts into the full flame of life – and the dog breeder therefore, if he be a true devotee of the sport of breeding, never fails to enjoy anew each time the thrill of ushering a new litter into the world of dogs and humans.

THE SIXTEEN PRINCIPLES OF DOG PEDAGOGY

1. All dog training must be founded upon "educating" the dog, that is, first drawing out of him and developing his instincts, and secondly, accidental and acquired abilities.
2. Situations and contacts must be interpreted entirely from the dog's, not the human's reactions and abilities.

3. The dog is not to be fooled. He has a sense of humiliation and of pride. If he has been taught to do a certain act, do not give him the command and then trifle with him. At all times let him see what you are doing.
4. Success must be at the completion of an act of training. The dog is to understand that at the end a certain thing will take place; for instance, if he is trailing, he must find the object trailed. Always he is to understand that when you say certain things, he is to do certain things, there must not be any break in this seeming cause and effect.
5. Commands should be given consistently in the same words and with the same tone of voice and speed of speaking.
6. Do not punish the dog for failures to obey unless you are certain that he understood fully what you commanded.
7. Give the dog a moment's time for carrying out your command. To demand instant obedience often is to confuse the dog.
8. Anticipate the dog's actions. Think ahead of him. Give your command not to step over a boundary line before he reaches the line.
9. If the dog does one step wrongly, do not repeat this step but begin again at the beginning for the dog must be taught to consider only successful acts in their entirety.
10. The dog has a single-track mind. Teach one specific thing at a time. This does not mean that

a training period can not include a half-dozen different tasks.

11. Reward should follow after every act done properly. Punishment should follow after every disobedience or failure.

12. Reward or punishment should follow quickly after the act. To punish a dog at any time other than instantly after the wrong act, is cruelty rather that part of training, for the dog, particularly a puppy, does not connect the punishment with the act.

13. Instruction should not be too long, as a dog, especially one under eight months, tires easily. An hour twice daily is sufficient length of time for special training work.

14. Try to locate each activity and command at or near the same location. If you call "brush," it should be at or near the place you groom the dog. This rule is based upon the law of association of ideas.

15. Do not lose your temper while training the dog. If you do, he loses some of his respect for you.

16. Have patience. The dog is not a human being. He probably is more successful as a dog than you are as a human being. His pleading liquid eyes and his wagging tail tell that he wants to do what you would have him do but that you are not as intelligent as he, else you would tell him in his language what you wish to say to him.

Photo] [*Sport and General.*

THE DUCHESS OF NEWCASTLE.

Her Grace is seen at the Joint Terrier Show in 1930 trying to make her Terrier, "Cracknels Verdict of Notts", show itself a little better. No one understands the Terrier better than the Duchess, and the present position of the breed is greatly due to her influence. The dog won eight first prizes.

EXTRACT

A swirl of gold-and-white and gray and black, -
Rackety, vibrant, glad with life's hot zest, -
Sunnybank collies, gaily surging pack, -
These are my chums; the chums that love me best.

Not chums alone, but courtiers, zealots, too,-
Clean-white of soul, too wise for fraud or sham;
Yet senseless in their worship ever new.
These are the friendly folk whose god I am.

A blatant, foolish, stumbling, purblind god,-
A pinchbeck idol, clogged with feet of clay!
Yet, eager at my lightest word or nod,
They crave but leave to follow and obey.

We humans are so slow to understand!
Swift in our wrath, deaf to the justice-plea,
Meting out punishment with lavish hand!
What, but a dog, would serve such gods as we?

Heaven gave them souls, I'm sure; but dulled the brain,
Les they should sadden at so brief a span
Of heedless, honest life as they sustain;
Or doubt the godhead of their master, Man.

Today a pup; tomorrow at life's prime;
Then old and fragile; -dead at fourteen years.
At best a meagre little inch of time.
Oblivion then, sans mourners, memories, tears!

Service that asks no price; forgiveness free
For injury or for injustice hard.
Stanch friendship, wanting neither thanks nor fee
Save privilege to worship and to guard:-

That is their creed. They know no shrewder way
To travel through their hour of lifetime here.
Would Man but deign to serve his God as they,
Millennium must dawn within the year.
- ALBERT PAYSON TERHUNE

GOOD DOGS

False friends, who love our gladsome hours,
In darksome days may flee;
But till our dogs deserters prove,
We cannot friendless be.

They love us still, through good and ill,
Through bright and stormy days;
And only ask, for service true,
One word of kindly praise.

For our dear sakes to shield and save,
Both fire and flood they brave;
They watch beside our dying-beds,
And mourn us at the grave.

The hero of a hundred fights
Has not his laurels won
By nobler deeds of courage high,
Than our good dogs have done!
- MRS. SURR

DOGS CAN BE TOUGHIES

The English press reports that a dog named Rex had been given up as dead on account of being buried in the debris of his master's home, that of W. J. Humphries, Birmingham, when an enemy bomb struck the house.

Six weeks later, as reported in the English Weekly Dog World: "Mr Humphries returned to the house to salvage what he could of his goods, and while searching among the wreckage, heard a whimper. With his bare hands Mr. Humphries began to dig and he found Rex lying helpless under the twisted remains of a bed. Rex could not stand for three days, but with careful attention he is recovering. It is hoped that he will pull through after his terrible experience."

The Editor has been criticized severely for stating in his various books that many dog owners are cruel to their dogs through the mistaken kindness of overfeeding them. Few dogs die of starvation; most dogs die indirectly through the contrary, being overfed and consequently acquiring digestive ills, which in turn lead on to vital illness.

MR. WALTER S. GLYNN'S CH. LAST O' REMUS
BY ROYSTON REMUS—BRYNHIR BLOSSOM.

THE DOG AS A WORD STUDY IN INTERNATIONAL ORTHOGRAPHY

The word dog in other languages is an interesting study of orthography.

Chinese – kou.
Danish, German, Norwegien – hund
French – chien
Hebrew – keleb
Irish – cu
Italian – cane
Japanese – inu
Belgian , Dutch – hond
Polish – pies
Russian – sobaka
Spanish – perro
Swedish – hundar
Czech – pes
Hungarian – kutya
Welsh – ki
Lithuanian – suo

REVENGE

Lo, when two dogs are fighting in the streets,
With a third dog one of the two dogs meets;
With angry teeth he bites him to the bone,
and this dog smarts for what that dog has done.

FIELDING

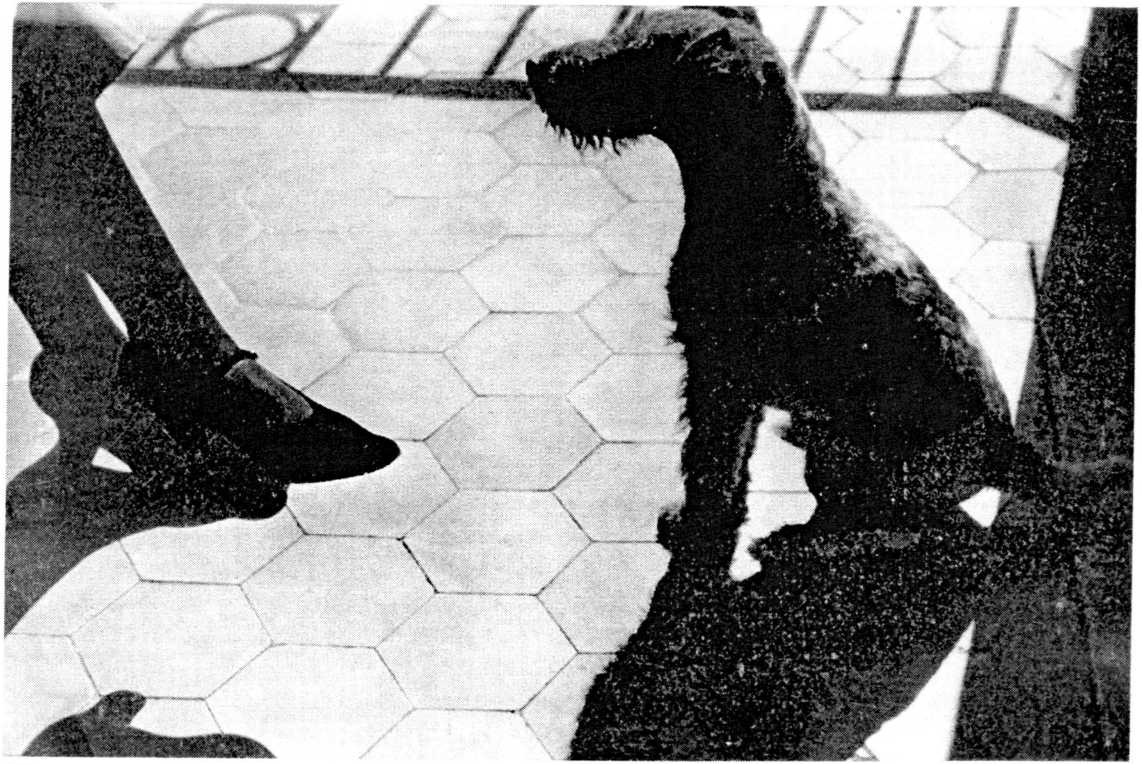

Dorien Leigh

A CANINE GENTLEMAN

[illegible]

TED

I have a little brindle dog,
Seal-brown from tail to head.
His name I guess is Theodore,
But I just call him Ted.

He's only eight months old to-day
I guess he's just a pup;
Pa says he won't be larger
When he is all grown up.

He plays around about the house,
As good as he can be,
He don't seem like a little dog,
He's just like folks to me.

And when it is my bed-time,
Ma opens up the bed;
Then I nestle down real cozy
And just make room for Ted

And oh, how nice we cuddle!
He doesn't fuss or bit,
Just nestles closely up to me
And lays there still all night.

We love each other dearly,
My little Ted and me.
We're just good chums together,
And always hope to be.

MR. T. J. STEPHENS' CH. SYLVAN RESULT

BY CH. CACKLEY OF NOTTS—ENCLOSURE.

Why the World Likes Dogs

THE MOST UNSELFISH living thing in the world is your dog. If you are in danger, your dog needs only to hear your cry of distress to rush to your aid, without thought of his own life, fearless of guns and enemies.

THE MOST PATIENT thing in the world is your dog, waiting for hours at the door to hear the sound of your footsteps, never complaining however late you may be.

THE MOST GRATEFUL thing in the world is your dog. Whatever you give him, whatever you do for him, he never is guilty of ingratitude. A pat of the hand, a soft-spoken word from you are golden pay. To him you are the most powerful personage in the world and beyond censure; you are your dog's god; you can do no wrong.

THE MOST FRIENDLY thing in the world is your dog. Of all the animal kingdom, he alone serves man without whip, without compulsion, glad to be by the side of his master wherever he may be, whatever he may do, and sad in heart when his master is away.

THE MOST FORGIVING thing in the world is your dog. The one virtue most humans lack is that of forgiveness. But your dog carries no grudge and no spite. Punish him even underservedly, and he comes to you, nudges his moist nose against your hand, lookds up at you with pleading eyes, and wags his tail hesitatingly as though to say, "Oh, come on, let's be pals again."

THE MOST LOYAL thing in the world is your dog. Whether you come home from Congress or from jail, whether you have lost your fortune or made a million, whether you return dressed in fashion's splendour or in wretched rags, whether you have been hailed hero or condemned as criminal, your dog is waiting for you with a welcoming bark of delight, a wagging tail and a heart that knows no guile.

The world likes dogs because dogs are nearest to moral perfection of all living things.

No Room in Heaven for Dogs

(An answer by the editor of Dog World to a letter from a 12-year old school boy)

I am sorry that your Sunday School teacher told you "there is no room in heaven for dogs." I can understand that this statement has disturbed you considerable.

Heaven is a big place because heaven is God and God stretches from the sun to the moon, to the stars, and back to earth.

Heaven must be a big place to hold all the good people who have died in the many years since the world began. As angels have wings, heaven must give them plenty of space in which to spread these wings and fly from one shifting cloud to another.

The millions upon millions of folks who have owned dogs and gone on to their heavenly home, surely would feel lonely without their dogs. And as there is no loneliness in heaven, God has made provision for man's best friend to dwell therein. We are certain of this, for it was God who named the dog by spelling His own name backwards.

Yes, heaven is a big place, with lots of shady spots, long lanes banked with flowers, fountains bubbling up out of the earth, good little rabbits munching on golden carrots, and by their side good dogs, big and little, dozing in the pure sunshine of celestial spaces.

It would be surprisingly strange, were there no dogs in heaven, for I believe that Christ had a little dog which followed him back and forth from Nazareth to Judea, through the streets of Jerusalem, and cuddled trustingly in the boat when He crossed the stormy sea of Galilee.

It seems to me I can see, on that tragic afternoon on Calvary, as Christ cried out "Why has Though forsaken me?", a little dog whining vainly at the foot of the cross to lick His bleeding hands. I believe that today this same little dog can be no other place than in heaven with Christ his master, lying contentedly at the foot of the throne of God.

I am sorry indeed that someone gave you the misinformation that "there is no room in heaven for dogs."

Photo] [*Metcalf.*

CH. "THET TETRARCH".

A good upstanding Terrier, bred and owned by Miss L. M. Dixon. A son of Ch. "Eden Aristocrat", it was a January puppy of 1929. He goes back to "Crusader".

Photo] [*Metcalf.*

"FLORNELL SALOON".

A well bred dog by Ch. "Talavera Simon", a son of the noted champion "Fountain Crusader". He goes back on both sides to "Barrington Bridegroom", considered by many to be one of the best Fox Terriers in the breed. "Saloon" is owned by Mr. Jim Parkington.

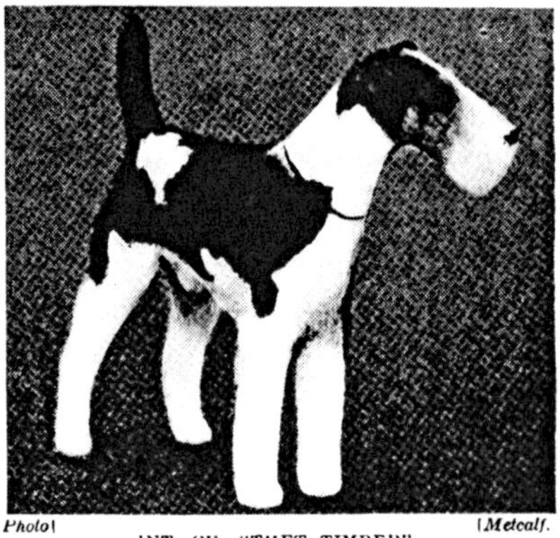

Photo] [*Metcalf.*

INT. CH. "THET TIMBER"

This outstanding dog was born in April of 1928. He was bred by Miss L. M. Dixon, whose kennel prefix is "Thet" His mother is "Simon's Dimple" "Thet Timber" is believed to hold a world's record as the only Wire Fox Terrier that is a champion of England, the United States and on the Continent.

WE ARE VICARS OF GOD

The Almighty created humans with the possibilities lurking within themselves of becoming godlike, approaching even to the Creator himself.

All other living things of the animal kingdom are termed the dumb creation or the lower animals. This term of inferiority is man-made and may not be in accord with the Creator's design of importance.

In primeval days the animals of the field and forest were on more nearly equal terms with the human animals. In this present age, with its myriads of inventions and machines, man has adjusted himself but the lower animals still retain mostly the capabilities of the primeval days, not having developed a language and a set of fingers and thumbs.

Therefore, the obligation is upon us to do for these living things that which they cannot do for themselves – to avoid unnecessary pain and suffering, to have opportunity to live their lives naturally and rear their young safely and to have the means of fulfilling their varying purposes in the plan of creation.

Surely we are only being appreciative of our status in the celestial scheme of things when we show consideration to all other living things and thereby, as it were, stand in the stead of the Creator.

It is for man, the allegedly superior animal, to show this superiority in kindness rather than force, in sympathetic understanding rather than brutal disregard.

We are vicars of God in this respect. Truly there is no surer way for the human soul to climb the heights than to have a constant, kindly regard for those considered as not having a soul or at best, an inferior one.

The Dog Issues 'His' Ten Commandments

1. Be sure you know more than I do before you attempt to teach and train me.
2. Look at my problems or any of your efforts to train me through my eyes and mind.
3. Don't become impatient with me until after you are certain I understand fully what you want me to do. Get your ideas across to me. Remember-I don't speak with words.
4. Don't lose your temper; it only makes you look weak and ridiculous to us dogs.
5. Make sure the water in my drinking pan is not stale, dust-filled, or unclean. Don't put anything in my drinking dish except clean, pure water.
6. I haven't hands for using brush and comb; so please groom me at least once every two days, else don't complain about canine body odour.

7. If I bark when I hear strange sounds, don't reprimand me too quickly. It is not easy for me to tell who is friendly and who is intent upon doing harm.
8. Give me a bit of notice when you approach me, especially if I am sleeping, or have my back turned.
9. On the street, keep tab on me, especially if I spy another dog across the street. Don't let me leave the curb.
10. Be proud of me as I am of you. And please, if I am ill, don't wait too long before you take me to my favourite veterinarian.

A PLEASING KIND OF INSANITY

That otherwise good people should travel the detour of a hobby and become abnormally zealous therein, at times to the detriment of their calling, is well known; but perhaps, it is not too well known that in this regard, indeed the most temperamental and seemingly fanatical are the dog breeders, the exhibitors at dog shows; and in general, all dog fanciers. Age is immaterial; the neophytes are as temperamental and high-strung as the old-timers.

They appear to be abnormal; they resent criticism; they extol their own dogs as the most desirable of all. Each one seeks the mirage of perfection in physical type, knowing full well that the perfect canine never exists – and so they learn to their disillusionment in the show ring time after time; but such defeats do not dampen their ardour through the years.

They carry on furiously and at times vociferously. They may even neglect their own money-making calling or permit it to suffer. They are strange folk; they argue with and against one another; they become mad competitors; yet in an instant, they shake hands, embrace each other and the losers congratulate the victor.

Indeed here is strange company! On the whole they are warm-hearted people; the subject of their hobby is a living, understanding thing; they deal in life itself; their obsession is not with ordinary live stock but with an animal which is said to come nearest to man in mental capabilities – namely, the dog, 'man's best friend,' so-called.

Yet notwithstanding all these things, we consider the dog people as warm-hearted and likeable folks tainted with a pleasing kind of insanity.

Photo| |*Hedges.*

"EDEN EXQUISITE".

It need hardly be said that the prefix "Crackley" stands for some of the very best in "Wires". This exceptionally good seven-and-a-half months old puppy was exported to the United States by Mr. J. R. Barlow. She has been considered one of the best bitch puppies seen.

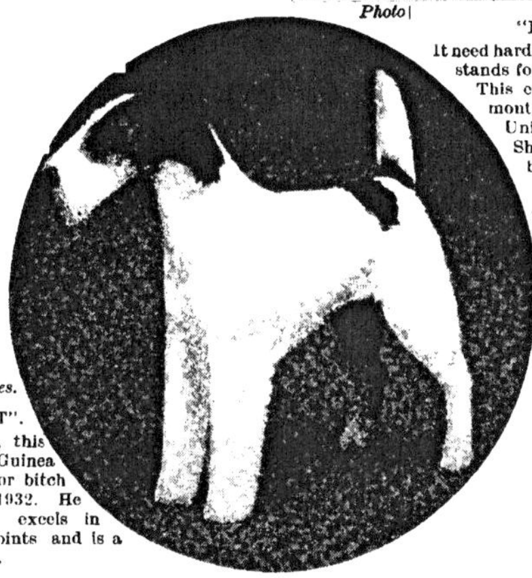

Photo| |*Hedges.*

CH. "FOURWENTS ROCKET".

Owned by Miss Joyce Esdaile, this winning dog won the Fifty Guinea Challenge Cup for the best dog or bitch at the Fox Terrier Club Show in 1932. He is a tan-marked headed dog, excels in bone, apart from other good points and is a son of "Dogberry Barbed Wire".

Photo| |*Hedges.*

INT. CH. "GALLANT FOX OF WILDOAKS".

This great Terrier, one of the best of recent times, was born in December of 1929, a son of Ch. "Crackley Supreme" out of a noted matron, Ch. "Gains Great Surprise", owned by Mrs. R. C. Bondy of New York. The latter is the mother of Ch. "Beau Brummel of Wildoaks".

Pity the Sick Dog

What is ahead for the sick animal in the fields? We all have seen a bird perched solemnly without motion for hours. Likely this bird is in the last stages of a disease which soon will drop it to the ground.

Just so with the old animal, the sick animal in the forest, and the dog that cannot protect itself against other dogs, that cannot go out and forage for its own food, where it must match cleverness and strength against that of its prey. Instead, it must lie quietly awaiting the end of life.

Pity the old dog, the sick dog, the crippled dog in the wilds!

"Faithful Barking Ghost"

"But in some canine Paradise
 Your wraith, I know, rebukes the moon.
And quarters every plain and hill,
 Seeking its master. As for me
 This prayer at least the gods fulfil
That when I pass the flood and see
Old Charon by Stygian coast
 Take toll of the shades who land,
Your little, faithful barking ghost
 May leap to lick my phantom hand!"
-St. John Lucas

MR. GEORGE RAPER'S CH. ST. ANN'S PRIMROSE

BY POULTON PLANET—BECKSIDE BEAUTY.

THE DIFFERENCE

My dog! The difference between thee and me
Knows only our Creator – only he
Can number the degrees in being's scale
Between th'Instinctive lamp, ne'er known to fail,
And that less steady light, of brighter ray,
The soul which animates thy master's clay;
And he alone can tell by what fond tie
My look thy life, my death thy sign to die.

No, when that feeling quits thy glazing eye
'Twill live in some blest world beyond the sky.
- ANONYMOUS

LITTLE LOST PUP

He was lost! – Not a shade of doubt of that;
For he never barked at a slinking cat,
But stood in the square where the wind blew raw,
With a drooping ear, and a trembling paw,
And a mournful look in his pleading eye,
And a plaintive sniff at the passer-by
That begged as plain as a tongue could sue,
"Oh, Mister, please may I follow you?"
A lorn, wee waif of a tawny brown
Adrift in the roar of a heedless town.
Oh, the saddest of sights in a world of sin
Is a little lost pup with his tail tucked in"

Well, he won my heart (for I set great store
On my own red Bute, who is here no more)
So I whistled clear, and he trotted up,
And who so glad as that small lost pup?

Now he shares my board, and he owns my bed,
And he fairly shouts when he hears my tread.
Then if things go wrong, as they sometimes do,
And the world is cold, and I'm feeling blue,
He asserts his right to assuage my woes
With a war, red tongue and a nice, cold nose.
And a silky head on my arm or knee,
And a paw as soft as a paw can be.

When we rove the woods for a league about
He's as full of pranks as a school let out;
For he romps and frisks like a three-months colt,
And he runs me down like a thunder-bolt.
Oh, the blithest of sights in the world so fair
Is a gay little pup with his tail in air!

- ANONYMOUS

MY DOG AND I

When living seems but little worth
And all things go awry,
I close the door, we journey forth –
My dog and I!

For books and pen we leave hehind,
But little careth he,
His one great joy in life is just
To be with me.

He notes by just one upward glance
My mental attitude,
As on we go past laughing stream
And singing wood.

The soft winds have a magic tough
That brings to care release,
The trees are vocal with delight,
The rivers sing of peace

How good it is to be alive!
Nature, the healer strong,
Has set each pulse with life athrill
And joy and song.

Discouragement! 'Twas but a name,
And all things that annoy,
Out in the lovely world of June
Life seemeth only joy!

And ere we reach the busy town,
Like birds my troubles fly,
We are two comrades glad of heart –
My dog and I!

- ALICE J. CLEATOR

Photo.] [Stanley M. Bathgate.

A FINE LOT.

Three positively delightful puppies by "Bowes Basil", a head study of which appears on page 677, were bred by Miss P. V. Lowe. It is impossible, at the age of three weeks, to say if a puppy will prove a winner, but heads such as are depicted above, are certainly a very good sign, as are such sturdy limbs.

Lost Dog

Whatever the cause of the dog being away from its accustomed surroundings, away from the humans it regards as godlike and indispensable, the mental pain of the dog must be intense.

Who at one time or another has not seen a dog running strangely along the street, terror in its eyes, its movements indicating total bewilderment? If one tries to be kindly-disposed to the dog, to speak a soft word, to seek to pat the dog, it looks up with a ray of hope in its eyes, then as it realizes the person is not the one he seeks, the pang is sharper than ever and the dog rushes away, block after block, until – well, one wonders what will be the ending – death under grinding auto wheels, the remainder of the years in heartsick separation, or perhaps at last the happy ending – reunited with owners and family.

Let us be realistic. In most cases the lost dog is lost because of the owner's negligence, either accidental or habitual. Keep your dog under control, worry about him, don't permit him out of your sight – better still, in public places have him on lead.

The too friendly dog is a likely victim of being lost, of being enticed away. It is a fine line to draw especially for the dog, between being too friendly and being wisely aloof. Do not permit strangers to be too friendly with your dog. I know this is strange advice but I believe it is wise advice.

Dognappers are doing their work constantly – despicable humans who snatch a beloved dog away, then scan the papers for reward offer. Dog thieves of course always are to be feared – those who steal dogs for sale to unscrupulous dog shops, to other individuals, or to laboratories and medical school classes.

IF YOUR DOG IS LOST, SOUND THE NEWS EVERYWHERE.

Scour the neighbour hood promptly. Ask all neighbours whether they have seen your dog. Ads in newspapers of course are a necessity. Visit the dog pound and the local animal shelter. If school is in session, ask the principal to post a notice. Offer a reward to the children; they all become zealous detectives.

Do not give up hope. Dogs have returned or been returned six months to a year after disappearance.

You should have an identification tag on the dog's collar – with phone number. Be able to describe your dog precisely for colour, makings, habits, size, etc. Always mention call name of dog.

Best of all, alert yourself and family before the dog has disappeared. A trained dog, properly controlled, is less apt to stray away and less apt to permit itself to be picked up.

MISS HATFEILD'S MORDEN BOMBARDMENT, MORDEN BLUSTERER, CH. DUSKY SIREN, CH. MORDEN BULLSEYE.

Photograph by Reveley, Wantage.

The Faith of a Dog

I've hunted the woodland and hill,
And "pointed" the quail in my day,
I could freeze as rigid and still
As a stone – when scent blew my way.
I recall the time you lost me
And I "pointed" the long hours through –
Though the night was too dark to see,
You came, as I knew you would do.
You gave me a pat in the darkness
And your voice was roughened and gruff –
But I knew by that one caress
That you understood well enough.
I'm just a dog but I love you,
And though I am stiffened and old –
My heart is as brave and as true,
My spirit still dauntless and bold.
I know that my hunting is done
I no longer gambol and bark –
But this one desire I have won,
Your hand on my head – in the dark!

MARGARET NICKERSON MARTIN
(blind poet)

Photo. [Sport and General.

"CHANDON COCKTAIL."

Observations of "Jay" upon the Five Great Wags. The Best Friends of Children and Men.

Dogs are the closest friends of children and men. Children come first for a dog's love, because of their understanding, and because dogs and children can but poorly tell of all that is in their hearts. Dogs have no words, and children but few.

The Boy has asked me to tell of some adventure in my life. But when I come to put the words down, I seem to think of no adventure which I care to speak of; for I am full of more serious matters. Besides, to tell of any of my great doings would take too much time. I do not want you to think that my life has been without strange and wonderful doings; that is not so – for it is crowded every day with many things worth telling. But I feel more like first letting you know of a dog's nature – his thoughts, pleasures, and feelings. I will do this; and some day I will speak of my "Great Fight with Uglymug," or my "Long Watch at the Door," or "How I Saved Boy," or "The Terrible Cat-Killing." (I was *blood wild* when I got into the last; so my good side shames me now.) These are a few of many adventures I have had. If the children really want me to, I will tell of any one, or all, some time.

Today I hear the wind blowing from the dear south into the tree-tops, the flies are making a singing sound, the sun is hot in spots on the ground, and many heavy smells come to my nose, each on with tempting colours. I sniff and sniff, and wish to shake myself hard and sharp, to drop the laziness off me, and go to seek adventures, not to tell of them. Today is a great tail-wagging time; so I must tell of the pleasure I have in it, and it may be when I get started on that subject I will speak of nothing else. I have a splendid tail for wagging purposes, and it is a constant joy and satisfaction to me.

First in the order of good wagging is the "Wag of deep love" for your Boy or Man friend. Of course, it is full of differences, according to the time of place, or Dog, but in the main it is the same, and Love is Love wherever the place be. So the wag is slow and sure from side to side and half-way in the air, never tight or rigid; it goes with ears neither back nor forward too far, and the eye-light is soft and appealing.

Second comes the "Great joy wag." This is begun with yaps, barks, whines away down in the throat, then jumps, runs, and licking of the hands, with violent wags every which way, all at once and well mixed up together. When you get a little settled down and sure the Master is there, well, happy, and loving you, you trot behind and smell his heel once in a while, or lick his hand to make him look at you. Then the last of the "joy wag" is to twist your body into a crook, as crooked as possible, and wag sidewise, stiff, and with little contented jerks. This is the dearest wag of all; a good dog loves it most, though it may not be so important as "deep love." It is felt all over the body and into the heart (dogs with bad dispositions cannot wag this way).

Third is the "Wag of alertness," and is used on many different occasions, but always when the mind is awake, keen, and watchful. This wag is somewhat hard to describe; for it is purely "dog," and needs understanding more than words to show what it means; but you can easily tell it, and know right well what it is. The wag may be seen when I am at a rat-hole, and is wagged to show that I know you are there and that I love you, but I do not want to be disturbed, or when I want to get after Jerry the cat, but don't dare, or when I see a stranger dog, that may be either friend or foe. To do this wag properly you must draw your tail up as high as possible, keeping it very stiff, then wag short and sharp, being careful to have no more on one side than the other; for it should become one-sided, you would lose grip of yourself, and appear undignified as well. The ears should be thrust sharply forward and never budged until things are settled or stiffness is no longer necessary.

Fourth – the "Dream wag." This one may not seem very important in the way of general wags, nor am I sure it should be fourth on the list, but it is to me very strange and interesting, leaving a great impression on my awakened mind. I carry a misty memory of it about with me when I am not very busy and on moonlight nights. There may be natural reasons for the "dream wag," – as, for instance, a fly on the ear where the hair is thin, too much heat from the fire, or a flea in the middle of your back, - but *I* think it is caused by going into another world, where wags change their methods and dogs speak with men's words. The Boy says my "dream wag" is queer and makes him afraid, and that I give hitchy jerks at the very end of my tail seven times, my jaws jerk and twitch, and my whine sounds far off in a very distant dog. I sometimes remember my dream; it is mixed –

pain, pleasure, and strangeness. I could tell you a dog-dream if I had time.

Fifth – Next comes the "Scratch wag." I might have left this one out, for some people will think it is not important; but it has always seemed to me that to get a pleasure without hurting anyone else or injuring yourself was perfectly right, and scratching your back hurts no one and gives you great happiness. The wag that goes along with this is almost any wag you care to make use of, varied in vigour according to the goodness or poorness of the scratching. I find that under the barn one can enjoy a fine continuous scratch in peace and quiet, if only the floor is neither too high nor too low and there are no green-eyed cats looking on. Then, there is a pleasant mystery and uncertainty about it all, and considerable satisfaction in knowing that no one sees how much fun you are having, or thinks you are a weak character because your wags are so mixed up with whines, growls, and throaty barks.

All that I have told you has been of the happy side of a dog's life, - that is, so far as his tail is concerned, - and I am loath to say anything of the *sixth* wag, which expresses all sorrow. But it may be that my words will sink deep into the heard of some boy, - so deep that he will never stand still unrebelling, when he sees a "fear wag." A dog's joy is blotted out by cruelty and abuse, and he is never the same again, having once been "cowed." Think of a *tail* wagging when he crawls along on his belly, twisting and squirming in trembling terror, with eyes full of fear and prayer! What would a smile upon your lips be, if terror and panic filled your heart, and your body drew together to receive a blow? When I see that sight I get the *blood fury*, and fear that some day I shall do terrible things to the coward of cowards, the low Man, who uses his mind and strength to flood a dumb creature's life with fear, and makes a tail to wag in cringing terror, when it should only be wagged for love, joy, and keen thinking.

I have now told you of the *five great waggings*, and the one wag of fear, which should not be counted, but still is sometimes seen. I have told of nothing else but wags, because wagging is of first importance. Of course, the tail is used in different ways by different dogs (but look out for the dog that never wags his tail, or has not tail). Wags and smiles make the heart kind. Barks, growls, yelps, and whines express a great deal, but I would give them all up rather than the "five waggings."

If the children want to know more about a dog's life, why he howls at the moon, growls in his sleep, loves to chase cats, hates some people, loves children – or anything of dogs' knowledge about dogs – let them ask me. Now the sun is soft and warm, the flies sing with their wings, streaks of blue smell come out of the woods and over the fields. I shall go to see what I may find. Wag joyfully! Good bye! Wag joyfully! Good bye!

- MORGAN SHEPARD

Photo] [*Hedges.*

CH. "CRACKLEY SURETHING".

This Wire-hair Terrier is one of Mr. J. R. Barlow's stud dogs standing in 1934 at a fee of six guineas, which will give the reader some idea on this matter. He is a son of Ch. "Crackley Startler" and was bred by Mr. K. A. Knight. He was born in 1932.

l
a
to

xercise
un behind
is necessary.
kind—that is to say
giving "gentle taps".
, just one which it will
acious, and, in the long

Photo] [*Hedges.*

CH. "TALAVERA PEGASUS."

The dog on the left is one of Captain H. R. Phipps' Terriers. He was born in July of 1930 and is a son of "Beau Brummel of Wildoaks", one of Mr. and Mrs. Bondy's famous dogs, exhibited both in England and in the United States.

Photo] [*Hedges*

CH. "TALAVERA JUPITER".

This well-known Terrier is also the property of Captain Phipps, and was bred by its owner, the sire being Ch. 'Beau Brummel of Wildoaks", which has thrown some remarkable stock both here and in America.

"Now I Have a Friend"

I had many friends in my lifetime-
Some who would borrow my very last dime;
I went through life, earned what I spent
Paid what I owed, lost what I lent.
My partner in business ran off with my wife,
Then stole my child and ruined my life,
The big bank failed where I kept my dough,
My house burned down, I had no place to go.
They all quit me cold when I could not lend.
So I bought me a dog – now I have a friend.

ANONYMOUS

An Outcast in Hell
(or the Dog Poisoner)

During a lull in the Stygian flames
    A group of shades were exchanging names,
And telling of places that they had been
    With bits of gossip and tales of sin.
A lonely shade who was standing by
    Approached to speak; but without reply
Each wrapped himself in his ghostly shawl!
    Murderers, robbers and blackguards all
With a whispered word and averted stare
    Vanished and left him standing there.
"Who was he?" I asked as they turned and fled.
    "He poisoned his neighbour's dog," they said.

ANONYMOUS

The Dog in the Library

So good you never knew that he was there
Until you came upon him in a nook
Beside the small grey woman as she searched
The well-known shelves for some yet unread
book.
He waited patiently as she would thumb
The leaves, and when she sauntered on he went
Pad-footed at her side, a little dog
Brown-patched, clean-white, devoted and
content.
Perhaps this dalliance bored him but he gave
No hint of tedium-no whimpered sound,
No tapping paws, no straining at the leash.
Only, at times when girls and boys would bound
Into the quiet place his eager eyes
Would follow them about the library,
And when swift choice they made and ran to play,
He seemed to watch their going wistfully.

ETHEL KING

CH. MATCHMAKER
Property of Messrs. Fraser & Lindsay, Canada

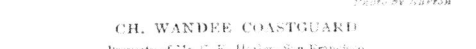

Photo by Reveley, Wantage

CH. DUSKY CRACKER
Property of Mr. F. Redmond, England

Photo by Barton

CH. WANDEE COASTGUARD
Property of Mr. C. K. Harley, San Francisco

Photo by Salmon, London

CH. DUSKY GLEANER
Property of Mr. F. Redmond, England

CH. HANDS UP
Late the property of Mrs. R. F. Mayhew

CH. BARKBY BEN
Property of Major G. M. Carnochan

THE BEST DOG

Yes, I went to see the bow-wows, and I looked at every one,
Proud dogs of each breed and strain that's underneath the sun;
But not one could compare with – you may hear it with surprise –
A little yellow dog I know that never took a prize.

Not that they would have skipped him when they gave the ribbons out,
Had they been a class to fit him – though his lineage is in doubt.
No judge of dogs could e'er resist the honest, faithful eyes
Of that plain little yellow dog that never took a prize.

Suppose he wasn't trained to hunt, and never killed a rat,
And isn't much on tricks or looks or birth – well, what of that?
That might be said of lots of folks whom men call great and wise,
As well as of that yellow dog that never took a prize.

It isn't what a dog can do, or what a dog may be,
That hits a man. It's simply this – does he believe in me?
And by that test I know there's not the compeer 'neath the skies
Of that plain little yellow dog that never took a prize.

Oh, he's the finest little pup that ever wagged a tail,
And followed man with equal joy to Congress or to jail.

I'm going to start a special show – 'Twill beat the world for size –
For faithful little yellow dogs, and each shall have a prize.
- ANONYMOUS

DOG LANGUAGE

Our Towser is the finest dog that ever wore a collar,
We wouldn't sell him – no, indeed – not even for a dollar!
I understand his language now, 'cause honest, it appears
That dogs can talk, and say a lot, with just their tails and ears.

When I come home from school he meets me with a joyous bound,
And shakes that long tail sideways, down and up, and round and round.
Pa says he's going to hang a rug beside the door to see
If Towser will not beat it while he's busy greeting me.

Then when he sees me get my hat, but thinks he cannot go,
His ears get limp, his tail drops sown, and he just walks off – slow;
Though if I say the magic words: "Well, Towser, want to come?"
Why, say! You'd know he answered "Yes," although at speech he's dumb.
- MARION HOVEY BRIGGS

By courtesy] [*C. H. Bishop.*

CH. "DUSKY SIREN"

An outstanding type of Terrier brought to the front by Miss Hatfield, then living at Morden, and who exhibited at the same time the noted "Dusky Cracker". "Siren" was born in 1903 and was painted by Maud Earl. It is interesting to compare this dog with some of the champions of to-day, but it must be borne in mind that the above picture is from a painting.

The Story of a Great Literary Gem

The world around, Senator Vest's Eulogy of the Dog is read and admired. Many varying stories have been written about the actual event, but a careful search of archives reveals the following, which the author assures is authentic.

On the front of the Old Courthouse in Warrensburg, Mo., a two-and-a-half story brink structure, no longer used, a bronze tablet bears this inscription:

"Within these walls on Sept. 23, 1870, Senator George Graham Vest delivered his famous eulogy on the dog. He died Aug. 14, 1904, and was buried in Bellefontaine Cemetery, St. Louis."

Old Drum, a black and tan coonhound owned by Charles Burden, was enjoying one of his usual trailing jaunts through the woods when a neighbour "Lon" Hornsby, redheaded and stubborn, shot Old Drum. However, it is to be noted that Hornsby, a reputable farmer and livestock rancher, had suffered the loss of more than 100 of his sheep during the few months previous.

On the evening of Oct. 28, 1869, Hornsby asked his companion, Richard Ferguson, to shoot the dog, as they detected Old Drum nearby in the twilight.

Burden filed a suit before the Justice of the Peace in Madison Township but the jury at the trial Nov. 25, 1869, failed to reach a decision and the case was set for retrial on the following Dec. 23.

Public feeling ran high on one side or the other and the second trial was well attended by farmers, cattle raisers and hunters of the area. Here Burden was awarded $25. Hornsby, his neighbour, appealed to Johnson Country Court of Common Pleas. This new trial, in March, 1870, with two attorneys on each side, brought a verdict in favour of Hornsby.

Burden, in turn, asked for and won a new trial. This fourth trial became a public mass meeting with the crowds overflowing the capacity of the courthouse.

The wagering on the outcome of the trial was about even up to the point when George Graham Vest of Phillips and Vest of Sedalia, Mo., attorneys for Burden, arose for the final argument for their client – this on Sept. 23, 1870.

Vest spoke for only a few minutes. The jury cam back promptly and returned the verdict in favour of Burden and Old Drum – for $50, twice the amount sued for originally.

Nine attorneys in all were connected with the case. One of them was David Nation, no other than the husband of the famous Carrie Nation. Elliott became judge of the Court of Common Pleas of Johnson County.

T. T. Crittenden later was elected governor of Missouri. Cockrell was a senator from that state for 30 years and afterward became a member of the Interstate Commerce Commission. John F. Phillips was appointed a commissioner of the Supreme Court of Mo. George Graham Vest was U.S. Senator from Mo. For 24 years.

CHAMPION GO BANG

CHAMPION THORNFIELD KNOCKOUT

Two good terriers formerly owned by Major G. M. Carnochan

Photo by Watson

THE GREAT MEERSBROOK BRISTLES

The most famous of all terrier sires. Imported and exhibited in America by Mr. C. W. Keyes, East Pepperell, Mass.

Senator Vest's Tribute to a Dog
THE TRIBUTE

THE BEST FRIEND a man has in the world may turn against him and become his enemy. His son or daughter that he has reared with loving care may prove ungrateful. Those who are nearest and dearest to us, those whom we trust with our happiness and our good name, may become traitors to their faith.

THE MONEY a man has he may lose. It flies away from him when he needs it most. A man's reputation may be sacrificed in a moment of ill-considered action. The people who are prone to fall on their knees to do us honour when success is with us, may be the first to throw stones of malice when failure settles its clouds upon our heads.

THE ONE absolutely unselfish friend that a man can have in this selfish world, the one that never deserts him, the one that never proves ungrateful or treacherous, is his dog.

A MAN'S DOG stands by him in prosperity and in poverty, in health and in sickness. He will sleep on the cold ground where the wintry winds blow and the snow drives fiercely if only he may be near his master's side. He will kiss the hand that has no food to offer, he will lick the sores and wounds that come in encounter with the roughness of the world. He guards the sleep of his pauper master as if he were a prince.

WHEN ALL other friends desert, he remains. When riches take wings and reputation falls to pieces, he is as constant in his love as the sun in its journey through the heavens.

IF MISFORTUNE drives the master forth an outcast in the world, friendless and homeless, the faithful dog asks no higher privilege than that of accompanying him to guard against danger, to fight against his enemies.

My Dog

Through glad days and sad days
    We two have clung together;
O'er rough roads and tough roads
    In every kind of weather.
Our square meals and spare meals
    Have both been shared together;
On warm nights and storm nights
    We've slept amongst the heather.
A fair friend, a rare friend
    Who never asks me whether
It's byways or highways
    Just so we are together.

WM. H. RUMSEY

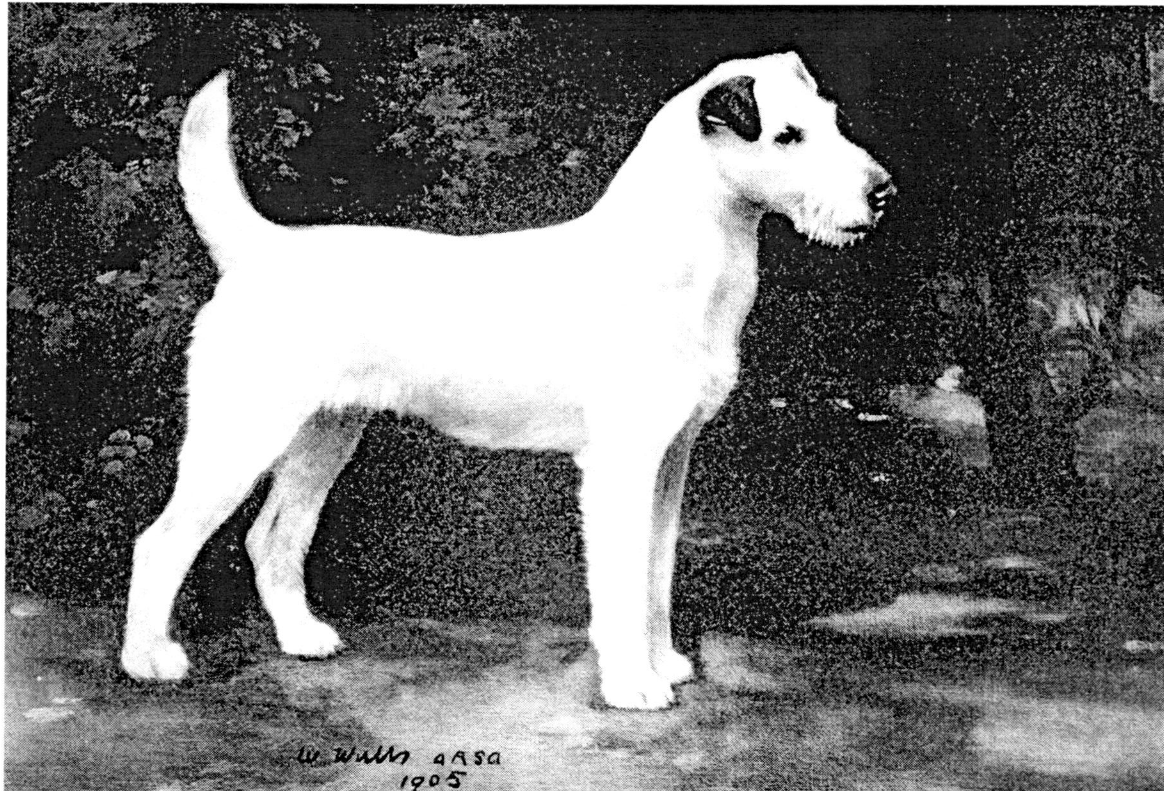

ey]

CH. "DUSKY REINE".

[C. H. E.

rly days of "Wires" Mr. Enfield showed the above dog, born in 1899, which was one of the best of the breed at that time. Smooth-coated Terrier breeders (for "Smooths" were then in fashion) considered "W
sh in the pan, only to discover they were mistaken. "Reine" was one of several noted winners that bore the prefix "Dusky", such as "Cracker", "Admiral", "Gleaner", and "Siren", the latter being shown on page

TRIBUTE TO DOG - 1200 A.D.

Nothing is more busy and wittier than a hound, for he hath more wit than other beasts.

And hounds know their own names, and love their masters, and defend the houses of their masters, and put themselves wilfully in peril of death for their masters, and run to take prey for their masters, and forsake not the dead bodies of their masters.

We have known that hounds fought for their lords against thieves, and were sore wounded, and that they kept away beasts and fowls from their masters' bodies dead. And that a hound compelled the slayer of his master with barking and biting to acknowledge his trespass and guilt.

The Power of the Dog

There is sorrow enough in the natural way
From men and women to fill our day;
But when we are certain of sorrow in store,
Why do we always arrange for more?
Brothers and sisters, I bid you beware
OF GIVING YOUR HEART TO A DOG TO TEAR!

We've sorrow enough in the natural way,
When it comes to burying Christian clay.
Our loves are not given, but only lent,
At compound interest at cent per cent.

Though it is not always the case, I believe,
That the longer we've kept 'em, the more we do grieve:
For, when debts are payable, right or wrong,
A short time loan is as bad as a long-
So why in Heaven (before we are there)
SHOULD WE GIVE OUR HEARTS TO A DOG TO TEAR?

Buy a pup and your money will buy
Love unflinching that cannot lie-
Perfect passion and worship fed
By a kick in the ribs or a pat on the head.
Nevertheless, it is hardly fair
TO RISK YOUR HEART FOR A DOG TO TEAR

When the fourteen years that Nature permits
Are closing in asthma, or tumour, or fits,
And the vet's unspoken prescription runs
To lethal chambers or loaded guns,
Then you will find-it's your own affair,
BUT...YOU'VE GIVEN YOUR HEART TO A DOG TO TEAR.

When the body that lived at your single will,
When the whimper of welcome is stilled (how still!);
When the spirit that answered your every mood
Is gone-wherever it goes-for good,
You will discover how much you care
AND WILL GIVE YOUR HEART TO A DOG TO TEAR.

Mr. G. M. Carnochan's (Riverdale-on-the-Hudson, New York)
CHAMPION "GO-BANG"

Dogs as Companions

They are much superior to human beings as companions. They do not quarrel or argue with you. They never talk about themselves but listen to you while you talk about yourself, and keep up an appearance of being interested in the conversation. They never make stupid remarks and they never ask a young author with fourteen tragedies, sixteen comedies, several farces, and a couple of burlesques in his desk, why he doesn't write a play.

They never say unkind things. They never tell us our faults, "merely for our own good." They do not at inconvenient moments mildly remind us of our past follies and mistakes.

They never inform us, like our inamoratas sometimes do, that we are not nearly so nice as we used to be. We are always the same to them. He is very imprudent, a dog is. He never makes it his business to inquire whether you are in the right or in the wrong, never bothers as to whether you are going up or down upon life's ladder, never asks whether you are rich or poor, silly or wise, sinner or saint. You are his pal. That is enough for him, and come luck or misfortune, good repute or bad, honour or shame, he is going to stick to you, to comfort you, guard you, give his life for you, if need be-foolish, brainless, soulless dog! – *Jerome K. Jerome* in Idle Thoughts Of An Idle Fellow.

Epitaph to a Dog

(On a monument in the garden of
Newstead Abbey, England)

NEAR THIS SPOT
ARE DEPOSITED THE REMAINS
OF ONE
WHO PSSESSED BEAUTY
WITHOUT VANITY,
STRENGTH WITHOUT INSOLENCE,
COURAGE WITHOUT FEROCITY,
AND ALL THE VIRTUES OF MAN
WITHOUT HIS VICES

THIS PRAISE, WHICH WOULD BE UNMEANING
FLATTERY
IFINSCRIBED OVER HUMAN ASHES,
IS BUT A JUST TRIBUTE TO THE MEMORY OF
"BOATSWAIN", A DOG
WHO WAS BORN AT NEWFOUNDLAND
MAY, 1803
AND DIED AT NEWSTEAD ABBEY
NOV. 18, 1808

When some proud son of man returns to earth,
Unknown to glory, but upheld by birth,
The sculptor's art exhausts the pomp of woe,
And storied urns record who rests below;
When all is done, upon the tomb is seen,
Not what he was, but what he should have been.
But the poor dog, in life the firmest friend,
The first to welcome, foremost to defend,

Whose honest heart is still his master's own,
Who labours, fights, lives breathes for him alone,
Unhonoured falls, unnoticed all his worth,
Denied in heaven the soul he held on earth-
While man, vain insect! hopes to be forgiven,
And claims himself a sole exclusive heaven.
Oh man! thou feeble tenant of an hour,
Debased by slavery, or corrupt by power-
Who knows thee well must quit thee with disgust,
Degraded mass of animated dust!
Thy love is lust, thy friendship all a cheat,
Thy smiles hypocrisy, thy words deceit!
By nature vile, ennobled but by name,
Each kindred brute might bid thee blush for shame.
Ye, who perchance behold this simple urn,
Pass on-it honours none you wish to mourn.
To mark a friend's remains these stones arise;
I never knew but one-and there he lies.

-LORD BYRON

Constancy

You don't need riches,
You don't need looks,
You needn't have read
A line in books,
You don't need purple,
You don't need fame-
Your dog will love you
Just the same!
You may lack money,
An ugly wight
Without the sense to
Come in at night,
You may be ragged,
And have no name-
Your dog will love you
Just the same!
-FRED B. MANN

A PROUD BOAST

I never barked when out of season;
I never bit without a reason;
I ne'er insulted weaker brother;
Nor wronged by force or fraud another.
Though brutes are placed a rank below,
Happy for man could he say so"
- BLACKLOCK

Little Dog Angel

High up in the courts of heaven today
        The little dog angel waits.
With the other angels he will not play
        But he sits alone at the gates.
For I know that my master will come, says he,
And when he comes he will call for me.
And his master, far in the world below,
        As he sits in his easy chair,
Forgets himself and whistles low
        For the dog-that is not there.
And the little dog angel cocks his ears
        And dreams that his master's voice he hears.
And I know, some day, when his master waits
        Outside in the dark and cold
For the hand of death to open the gates
        That lead to those courts of gold,
The little dog angel's eager bark
Will comfort his soul while he's still in the dark.

-NORAH M. HOLLAND

THE DOGLESS BOY

"But the poor dog, in life the firmest friend,
The first to welcome, foremost to defend.
Whose honest heart is still his master's own,
Who labours, fights, lives, breathes for him alone."
BYRON

Boy is used here in a generic sense, for the love of animals, and especially dogs, is not confined to either sex. We do not think a boy was ever born who, if "entered" properly, would not love a dog and when given the opportunity. There seems to be some affinity between children and dogs. The selfish cat may be a family pet, but its horizon of affection is usually filled with a warm fireside and a saucer of milk and the claws within the velvet are typical of its nature; uncertain of temperament and cruel even in its seeming play. Not so the dog. It matters not whether his lineage proclaims him a blue blood or a mongrel, there is something behind the eye of a dog which draws to the heart. No animal is so responsive to the humanizing effect as the dog. His idiosyncrasies and temperament are, like those of man, much a matter of environment. Cuff him and treat him generally as an Ishmael and he becomes one, treat him like so many are in kennels nowadays, as a mere chattel to be housed and fed as one of a number and he becomes a mere automaton; but treat him as a friend, as one of your household an dhow soon the human influence is marked. His ideas are widened, his intelligence develops and the many beautiful traits of a confiding, honest nature which have earned him the title of man's best friend, are brought to the surface. Though the society of man has a humanizing effect on our four-footed friends, the dog himself in no less manner, through his transparent temperament and honest actions may suggest and encourage the same traits in the budding nature of his little friend. Every boy should own a dog. Josh Billings well said that in the whole history of the world there is but one thing that money cannot buy, to wit: "The wag of a dog's tall." He might have added there is no animal on God's earth who, in the honesty of his affection, will still love and wag his tail for the hand which beats him. The love of Bill Sykes' dog for his brutal master is one of the sublimest thoughts Dickens ever conceived.

The boy who is raised with a dog for a "pal" is unwittingly humanized. The love for another is engendered in his heart, and afterward has its effect on his conduct in the wide world of mankind. Be his nature cruel, more from thoughtlessness than any inherent feeling, if he is a lad worth his salt he cannot but learn a lesson from the mild reproach of the brute he torments.

A horse would kick, a cat would bite or scratch under the same provocation; not so the dog. There are exceptions, of course, but no dog, we believe, is born savage; if he develops bad temper it is generally due to environment, and the parent's judgment must be exercised in providing the right sort of dog for the boy, as in other provisions for his welfare. A man may become a lover of dogs when manhood's cares and responsibilities place the dog on the same level as a favourite pipe. He has missed something. He will not "get into" his dog as he would have done as a boy. Once a dog lover always a dog lover, no matter whether the circumstances of his after life compel him to love them from afar. The dog is the better for it and so is the man. Buy your son a dog. – H. W. L.

Photo] [*E. C. Ash.*

"BOWES BREVITY".

This soundly built Terrier, bred by Mr. A. T. King, is a half brother to the noted Ch. "Petwick Cocktail", the property of Mr. H. L. Cottrill. "Brevity" is the sire of over 100 winners, including two champions, and was second best stud dog at the Wire Fox Terrier Show. Unfortunately, the dog having been tampered with, his show career was ended early, the culprit never being discovered.

Pals

Hurrah!
Here they come!
Heralded loud by fife and drum,
The Boy and his Pal in proud parade!
The Boy is nonchalant, unafraid,
Heir of the Ages! Fronting life,
Ready to tilt with toil and strife.
And the Pal? He keeps his chum in sight,
Barking to left and barking to right,
And the two, as they march, proclaim to all,
"We are Boy and Dog, and Pal and Pal!"
Hurrah!
Watch them jog!
Wonderful creatures! Boy and Dog!

-SUSIE. H. BEST

The Little Black Dog

I wonder if Christ had a little black dog,
All curly and woolly like mine,
With two long silk ears and a nose round and wet,
And two eyes brown and tender that shine.
I'm sure if He had, that little black dog
Knew right from the first He was God,
That he needed no proof that Christ was divine,
But just worshipped the ground He trod.

I'm afraid that He hadn't, because I have Read Books
How He prayed in the Garden alone,
When all of His friends and disciples had fled,
Even Peter, that one called a stone.
And oh, I am sure that little black dog
With a true heart so tender and warm
Would never have left Him to suffer alone,
But creep right under His arm;
Would have licked those dear fingers in agony clasped,
And counting all favours but loss,
When they led Him way, would have trotted behind
And followed Him quite to the cross.
-ELIZABETH GARDNER REYNOLDS

Proverbs and Bits of Wisdom about Dogs

The more I see of men, the better I like my dog – FREDERICK THE GREAT *(of his Italian greyhound).*

"God created man; then seeing how weak he was, gave him the dog." –TOUSSENEL.

For my part, I do with thou wert a dog, that I might love thee. – SHAKESPEARE

Whenever a man is unhappy, God sends him a dog.
-LAMARTINE

Dog is the only animal that loves you more than he loves himself – OLD SAYING

EPITAPH FOR A SMALL DOG

Here rests a little dog
Whose feet ran never faster
Than when they took the path
Leading to his master
-LEBARON COOKE

EPITAPH ON A FAVOURITE DOG

Thou who passest on the path; if haply thout dost mark this monument, laugh not I pray thee, though it is a dog's grave; tears fell for me and the dust was heaped above me by a master's hands who likewise engraved these words on my tomb. – *From Greek literature (about 350 B.C)*

EPITAPH ON A DOG'S TOMBSTONE NEAR CHEVY CHASE, M.D., (1940)

"Dear Master:

I've explained to St. Peter, I'd rather stay here, outside of the pearly gates. I won't be a nuisance, I won't even bark. I'll be very patient and wait. I'll lie here and chew a celestial bone, no matter how long you may be. I miss you so much. If I went in alone, it wouldn't be heaven for me."

Photo. [*Sport and General.*

WIRE-HAIRED FOX TERRIERS.

Authorities seem to agree that the wire-haired black and tan was Britain's first Terrier, and there can be little doubt that the Wire-haired Fox Terrier owes its origin to it. A few years ago the smooth Fox Terriers were far more prized than their rough-coated relations, but recently the wire-haired has come into its own and now this engaging companion is by far the most popular of all Terriers. The two shown here are "Petwick Courtesan" and "Petwick Cointreau", bred by Mr. H. L. Cottrill.

WHEN THE DOG'S SOUL COMES THROUGH HIS EYES

If a man does not soon pass beyond the thought "By what shall this dog profit me?" into the large state of simple gladness to be with dog, he shall never know the very essence of that companionship which depends not on the points of dog, but on some strange and subtle mingling of mute spirits. For it is by muteness that a dog becomes for one so utterly beyond value. With him one is at peace where words play no torturing tricks. When he just sits loving and knows that he is being loved, those are the moments that I think are precious to a dog: when, with his adoring soul coming through his eyes, he feels that you are really thinking of him.

– JOHN GALSWORTHY in Memories.

HOW BENVENUTO CELLINI'S DOG IDENTIFIED A ROBBER

Happening just about this time to pass by the square of Navona with my fine shock-dog, as soon as I came to the door of the city marshal, the dog barked very loudly and flew at a young man, who had been arrested by one Donnino, a goldsmith of Parma, formerly a pupil of Caradosso, upon suspicion of having committed a robbery. My dog made such efforts to tear this young fellow to pieces that he roused the city-guards.

The prisoner asserted his innocence boldly, and Donnino did not say so much as he ought to have done, especially as I was present. There happened likewise to be by one of the chief officers of the city-guard, who was a Genoese, and well acquainted with the prisoner's father; insomuch that on account of the violence offered by the dog, and for other reasons, they were for dismissing the youth, as if he had been innocent.

As soon as I came up, the dog, which dreaded neither swords nor sticks, again flew at the young man. The guards told me that if I did not keep off my dog they would kill it. I called off the dog with some difficulty, and as the young man was retiring, certain little paper bundles fell from under the cape of his cloak, which Donnino immediately discovered to belong to him.

Amongst them I perceived a little ring which I knew to be my property: whereupon I said: 'This is the villain that broke open my shop, and my dog knows him again.' I there fore let the dog loose, and he once more seized the thief, who then implored mercy, and told me he would restore me whatever he had of mine. On this I again called off my dog, and the fellow returned me all the gold, silver, and rings that he had robbed me of, and gave me five-and-twenty crowns over, imploring my forgiveness.

–BENVENUTO CELLINI
(from *Memoirs*, ending in 1562)

Rip Van Winkle's Dog Wolf

Rips sole domestic adherent was his dog Wolf, who was as much henpecked as his master; for Dame Van Winkle regarded them as companions in idleness, and even looked upon Wolf with an evil eye as the cause of his master's going so often astray. True it is, in all points of spirit befitting an honourable dog, he was as courageous an animal as ever scoured the woods – but what courage can withstand the ever-during and all-besetting terrors of a woman's tongue?

The moment Wolf entered the house, his crest fell, his tail drooped to the ground, or curled between his legs, he sneaked about with a gallows air, casting many a sidelong glance at Dame Van Winkle, and at the least flourish of a broomstick or ladle, he would fly to the door with yelping precipitation. . .

Poor Rip was at last reduced almost to despair, and his only alternative to escape from the labour of the farm and clamour of his wife, was to sometimes take gun in hand, and stroll away into the woods. Here he would sometimes seat himself at the foot of a tree, and share the contents of his wallet with Wolf, with whom he sympathized as a fellow-sufferer in persecution. 'Poor Wolf,' he would say, 'thy mistress leads thee a dog's life of it; but never mind, my lad, whilst I live thou shalt never want a friend to stand by thee"' Wolf would wag his tail, look wistfully in his master's face, and if dogs can feel pity, I verily believe he reciprocated the sentiment with all his hear.

– WASHINGTON IRVING (from *Rip Van Wingle,* in *The Sketch Book)*, 1820.

From the painting by] [*Ward Binks*

WIRE-HAIRED FOX TERRIERS

THE DOG UNDER THE WAGON

"Come, wife," said good old farmer Gray,
"Put on your things, 'tis market day,
And we'll be off to the nearest town,
There and back ere the sun goes down.
Spot? No, we'll leave old Spot he whined,
And soon made up his doggish mind
          To follow under the wagon.

Away they went at a good round pace
And joy came into the farmer's face,
"Poor Spot," said he, "did want to come,
But I'm awful glad he's left at home –
He'll guard the barn, and guard the cot,
And keep the cattle out of the lot."
"I'm not so sure of that," thought Spot,
          The dog under the wagon.

The farmer all his produce sold
And go his pay in yellow gold:
Home through the lonely forest. Hark!
A robber springs from behind a tree;
"Your money or else your life," said he;
The moon was up, but he didn't see
          The dog under the wagon.

Spot ne'er barked and Spot ne'er whined
But quickly caught the thief behind;
He dragged him down in the mire and dirt,
And tore his coat and tore his shirt,
Then held him fast on the miry ground;
The robber uttered not a sound,

While his hands and feet the farmer bound,
And tumbled him into the wagon.

So Spot he saved the farmer's life,
The farmer's money, the farmer's wife,
And now a hero grand and gay,
A silver collar he wears today;
Among his friends, among his foes –
And everywhere his master goes –
He follows on his horny toes,
The dog under the wagon.

- ANONYMOUS

QUESTIONS

Is there not something in the pleading eye
Of the poor brute that suffers, which arraigns
The law that bids it suffer? Has it not
A claim for some remembrance in the book
That fills its pages with the idle words
Spoken of man? Or is it only clay,
Bleeding and aching in the potter's hand,
Yet all his own to treat it as he will,
And when he will to cast it at his feet,
Shattered, dishonoured, lost for evermore?
My dog loves me, but could he look beyond
His earthly master, would his love extend
To Him who – hush! I will not doubt that He
Is better than our fears, and will not wrong
The least, the meanest of created things.

- OLIVER WENDELL HOLMES

A FRIENDLY WELCOME

'Tis sweet to hear the watch-dog's honest bark
Bay deep-mouthed welcome as we draw near home;
'Tis sweet to know there is an eye will mark
Our coming, and look brighter when we come.
- LORD BYRON

TO A DOG

On every side I see your trace;
Your water-trough's scarce dry;
Your empty collar in its place
Provokes the heavy sigh.

And you were here two days ago.
There's little changed, I see.
The sun is just as bright, but oh!
The difference to me!

The very print of your small pad
Is on the whitened stone.
Where, by what ways, or sad or glad,
Do you fare on alone?

Oh, little face, so merry-wise,
Brisk feet and eager bark!
The house is lonesome for your eyes,
My spirit somewhat dark.

Now, small, invincible friend, your love
Is done, your fighting o'er,
No more your wandering feet will rove
Beyond your own house-door.

The cats that feared, their hearts are high,
The dogs that loved will gaze
Long, long ere you come passing by
With all your jovial ways.

Th'accursed archer who has sent
His arrow all too true,
Would that his evil days were spent
Ere he took aim at you!

Your honest face, your winsome ways
Haunt me, dear little ghost,
And everywhere I see your trace,
Oh, well-beloved and lost!

- ANONYMOUS

WIRE-HAIRED FOX TERRIERS—SIR DANIEL AND MISS JUNE, the property of Mrs. Wadd, Fairhope, Richmond Hill, Surrey. Notice the typical head and front legs.

As a sporting breed, the Fox Terrier is equal to any. It seems born in their small souls, the 'I-can't-be-beaten-nohow' spirit, and they are usually very surprised if they learn that stronger fiercer things do actually exist.

Dr. Caius describes the Terrier as one 'which hunteth the fox and the Badger or Greye only! whom we call Terrars because they (after the manner and custome of Ferrets in searching for Connyes) creep into the grounde and by that meanes make afrayde, nyppe and bite' . . . !—*Fleming's Translation.*

A BOY AND A DOG

I want my boy to have a dog
Or maybe two or three
He'll learn from them much easier
Than he would learn from me.
A dog will show him how to love
And bear no grudge or hate
I'm not so good at that myself
But dogs will do it straight.
I want my boy to have a dog
To be his pal and friend
So he may lean that friendship
Is faithful to the end.
There never yet has been a dog
Who learned to double-cross
Nor catered to you when you won
Then dropped you when you lost.

-Mary Hale, *The Old Spinner*

THROUGH SUNLIT FIELDS

(Poetical Reverie of a "Bird Dog" Man)

Through sunlit fields I sometimes stride
My stalwart pointers by my side.
The joy of life sings through each vein,
Who would not thrill to its refrain
While carefree roaming meadows wide,
The fall is o'er and now betide
On city sidewalks I must stride,
No more my pointers dash amain
Through sunlit fields.
But when in winters even'tide
I loll and doze by fire beside,
Imagination has free rein
And then I see myself again,
On mem'ries magic carpet ride
Through sunlit fields.

-EDWARD DANA KNIGHT

FOR A LITTLE BOY

I want to give a little boy-such an important little boy-something that will show him FAITH, alive and glowing.

I want to give a little boy something that will teach the spirit of him the glorious virtue of unselfish COURAGE.

I want to give a little boy something that will impress upon his clean heart and spirit every day, every night, every hour of the day and night the mighty power and exquisite beauty of LOVE.

I want to teach a little boy the importance of, and the reason for, DISCIPLINE.

And so=I am going to give a little boy a little dog, and what a gay and happy time a little boy and a little dog and a devoted dad will have! What a lovely and fascinating and interesting school we will attend-we three together! – R. A. Grady

AMORA, WIRE-HAIRED TERRIER.

"CHILDREN-DOG RECIPE"

Take on large grassy field,
One half-dozen children,
Two or three small dogs,
A pinch of brook
And some pebbles –

Mix the children and dogs, well together, then put them in the field, stirring constantly. Pour the brook over the pebbles. Sprinkle the field with flowers. Spread over all a deep blue sky, and bake in the hot sun. When brown, remove and set away in a bathtub to cool.

–Author unknown.

WHEN CAESAR MARCHED BEHIND HIS KING

When were kings compelled to march behind a dog?

When King Edward VII of England died in 1910, it was learned he had given stern instructions that his pet fox terrier named Caesar march directly behind the artillery caisson carrying his body. Edward even threatened to haunt any one who disobeyed this order.

And so it happened – Caesar marched behind his master's body; and kings, potentates, prime ministers and Emperor Kaiser Wilhelm of Germany marched behind the little terrier.

Caesar himself lived to the ripe age of 14 years and was buried in a bronze casket at Fort Rudd, England.

ON THE ESSENTIAL ATTRIBUTES OF A DOG OWNER

Great Britain has an international reputation of being a nation of animal lovers. As recent statistics estimate the canine population of Britain to be approximately three million, while registrations at the Kennel Club are now in the region of 100,000 per year, there can be little doubt that we are a nation of dog owners. It is a sad fact, however, that in many cases these dogs are kept by owners who are far from being true animal lovers. It is still necessary for us to have a very active Royal Society for the Prevention of Cruelty to Animals; a fact which has often been commented upon to the writer by people abroad.

Happily, however, cases of downright physical cruelty to dogs, and to other animals, are rare in this country; but it is surprising how ignorant the average dog owner is, and the amount of cruelty through ignorance – incorrect, and over-, feeding, bad housing, continual "doseing", and insufficient exercise – to dogs is appalling. Many owners who would never beat a dog, and who would be most indignant if the truth was told them, are cruel to their dogs by habitually over-feeding them emotionally, as well as physically. There are also such thoughtless cruel acts as permitting small children to torment a dog, even if not inflicting physical pain, when the animal is not inclined to play.

This unconscious cruelty on the part of dog owners can be easily overcome by learning the correct principles of dog management, and an intelligent application of these principles without undue fussiness and sentimentality.

In becoming a dog owner certain responsibilities are undertaken, and the owner *must* be prepared to sacrifice something, if only in time and trouble, to the well-being of his pet, in the same way that married couples have to sacrifice a good deal of their pleasure when they undertake the responsibility of children.

It may be possible to keep a dog properly and in good health even in a bed-sitting room, provided one has the time to take him out, and in these circumstances it will be necessary much more frequently than with a dog kept in a large house with free access to a garden – but it would obviously be cruelty to keep, say, a large gun-dog under such conditions. If circumstances do not permit of a dog being kept properly, it is the *real* dog lover who refrains from keeping a dog until conditions change.

A sympathetic understanding of the dog – sloppy sentimentalism is *not* meant by this – is in-born in some people and can never be acquired by others, but it is possible for anyone to develop this to some extent or other. This is done by observation, a sensible love of dogs without undue "sloppiness", firmness without harshness, and by acquiring the knack of getting inside a dog's mind and understanding things from the dog's point of view. It is imperative that the dog's respect and trust should be gained by the owner; unfairness is a thing with a dog cannot understand and will never forgive. Unlimited patience and the strictest temper control on the part of the owner are essential, as are reliability, scrupulosity, regularity and method.

The ignorance on the part of dog owners, to which reference has been made, can best be overcome by practical instruction under a master of the subject, who, in addition, can impart his knowledge. As a practical course in dog management cannot possibly be undertaken by the majority of ordinary dog owners, the only alternative for them is to acquire as much knowledge as possible from books. But here a word of warning is necessary – it is essential that books on dogs should be read, and the advice given in them applied, with common sense. No book ever written can mention every possible contingency, and details vary with cases, but principles never vary, and if one has a good knowledge of sound principles of dog management and has taken the pains to develop the other attributes necessary in a dog owner, they can themselves readily adapt details to circumstances, and thereby give a fair deal to mankind's most responsive of companions – the Dog.

In a handbook of this nature, on a subject so large, it is only possible to give a brief outline; but it is to be hoped that the general facts explained will enable the owner to develop a sympathetic understanding of hi dog and the desire to seek more detailed knowledge from experienced friends, and from larger and more specialized books on the various aspects of dog management.

- CHARLES CASTLE

MISS GUEST'S RANÊE, WIRE-HAIRED TERRIER.

DOGS ON THE ROMAN FARM

Nor let the care of dogs be last in your thoughts; feed swift Spartan whelps and fierce Molossians alike on fattening whey. Never, which them on guard, need you fear in your stalls a midnight thief, nor onslaught of wolves, nor restless Spaniards behind your back. – Virgil – (From the *Georgies* III, trans. H. R. Fairclough), 30 B.C.

WHAT BREED WAS IT?

There is a certain strong breed of hunting-dogs, small, but worthy of a sublime song, which the wild tribes of painted Britons maintain, and they call them gaze-hounds. Their size, indeed, is about that of the worthless pampered domestic tabledogs, crooked, slight, shaggy, dull-eyed, but furnished with numerous envenomed teeth, and their feet armed with formidable nails.

The gaze-hound excels above all in his nose; he is first-rate for tracing, since he is very sagacious in finding the track of animals over the ground, and moreover, expert in indicating the very odour that floats in the air. –Oppian of Apamea (from *Cynegetica*, C. 215 A.D.)

'AWAY FROM CIVILIZATION, WHAT DOES ONE NEED MOST?'

If I had to spend a long time away from civilization and could take only one thing with me I would certainly take something alive, preferably a dog.

The reasons for this are because of his unwavering loyalty, his sense of responsibility as regards his master's person and belongings, his extremely acute sense of approaching danger and the absolute adoration that even a mongrel is capable of giving his owner.

More than anything alive, the dog seems to fill the need of a close affectionate honest friend. Therefore I would take a dog.

There is nothing in his mechanism to go static. There is nothing forced or mechanic about his feeling for you. There is no danger which hw ill not share willingly. He will never be disgustingly drunk. Neither will insist upon talking when you desire quiet. And no matter how soundly he may seem to be sleeping – if you need him he is right there every time.

I would take a dog because if, away from civilization, death should chance to be my lot, I could pass on happier in the knowledge that while life remained in his faithful body my dog would still be my champion, my defender. I am sure I would sleep the sweeter knowing that he was lying above me whispering "Peace, old pal, on the long, long trek."

"ON THE SLY"

One thing my wife and I've said over
And over-we will not feed Rover
At table, even though he begs
And nuzzles up against our legs
And toward us is forever turning
Those looks of hunger, hurt, and yearning...
We have agreed and that is why
We only do it on the sly.

-RICHARD ARMOUR.

THE HOME-LOVING DOG

The lonely fox roams far abroad,
On secret rapine bent, and midnight fraud;
Now haunts the cliff, now traverses the lawn,
And flies the hated neighbourhood of man:
While the kind spaniel, or the faithful hound,
Likest that fox in shape and species found,
Refuses through these cliffs and lawns to roam,
Pursues the noted path, and covets home;
Does with kind joy domestic faces meet,
Take what the glutted child denies to eat,
And, dying, licks his long-loved master's feet.

WIRE FOX TERRIER

LOYALTY

(Reprinted from Dog World, 1924)

A man may lose his house and lot,
His friends may pass him by,
He may not have a thin dime left
To rent a slab of pie;

But if he owns the homeliest
And saddest dog in town,
He has one pal whose honest love
Will never turn him down.

A man may kick his mangy pup
And cuss him day and night,
Still will the faithful cur be true
And greet him with delight.

Life long he sits upon the porch
And wags his happy tail,
To greet his lord when he shall come
From Congress or from jail.

WIRE FOX TERRIER

THIS ILLUSTRATION IS TO SHOW THE WONDERFUL IMPROVEMENT THAT HAS TAKEN PLACE WITHIN RECENT YEARS OF THE PRESENT TYPE OF WIRE-HAIRED FOX-TERRIERS AS COMPARED WITH THE ABOVE

LIKE CHILD, LIKE PUPPY

Owning a dog is a serious responsibility. To enjoy the position of dog's master incurs obligation. The dog surrenders many of his natural rights and habits in return for the servitude he gives the human.

The puppy is the perfect example of trusting loyalty. To him the world's a stranger to be greeted. Not only each day but each moment of each hour of the day, he discovers something new in our world of humans, in which he must live.

Life is an endless chain experience of play, discovery and thrills. Not a care worries his carefree soul. What scene on this earth holds more pure happiness than that of a litter of playing puppies – brothers and sisters in a family world that has not yet known separation!

Consequently, a puppy, particularly if it is brought into a new home, should receive every consideration in the way of feeding, care, housing and training. At three months of age, it compares with the infant just out of the cradle; and to a great extent the same care which the child receives, should be given to the puppy.

Old Type of Wire-Haired Fox-Terrier—Mr. Carrick's Carlisle Tack (late Tack).

GREAT FRIEND MAKER

Dale Carnegie, whose book How to Make Friends and Influence People has been a best seller, write: 'Why read my book to find out how to win friends?" Why not study the technique of the greatest winner of friends the world has ever known? You may meet him coming down the street. When you get within ten feet of him he will begin to wag his tail. If you stop and pat him he will almost jump out of his skin to show how much he likes you.

And you know that behind this show of affection on his part, there are no ulterior motives; he has nothing to sell and doesn't want to marry you.

"Did you ever stop to think that a dog is the only animal that does not have to work for a living? A hen has to lay eggs; a cow has to give milk; and a canary has to sing. But a dog makes his living by giving you nothing but love."

WALKING WITH A DOG HAS EXTRA PLEASURE

You will generally fare better to take your dog than invite your neighbour.

Your dog is a true pedestrian, and your neighbour is very likely a small politician. The dog enters thoroughly into the spirit of the enterprise; he is not indifferent or preoccupied; he is constantly sniffing adventure, laps at every spring, looks upon every field and wood as a new world to be explored, is ever on some fresh trail, knows something important will happen a little farther on, gazes with the true wonder-seeing eyes, whatever the spot or whatever the road, finds it good to be there – in short, is just that happy, delicious, excursive vagabond that touches one at so many points, and whose human prototype in a companion robs miles and leagues of half their power to fatigue. – JOHN BURROUGHS.

IF YOU CAN'T FIND THE PERFECT MAN, OWN A DOG

"And there is more than one woman – even a beautiful woman – who has never found the man to love the pilgrim soul in her; and, after passionate protestations and broken vows, old, disillusioned, sad, and deserted, she has regained faith in love and fidelity through the devotion of a dog.

"He does not change when beauty flees, nor when poverty comes, nor when health goes. He gives his heart, his true and single heart to his mistress forever.

"She may be old and grey, with furrowed face, but he sees the pilgrim soul in her. "

– Mrs. T. P. O'Connor in her book Dog Stars.

Type of Wire-Haired Fox-Terrier—Mr. J. D. Dudson's Champion Briar Sportsman.

WHEN DACHS' EYES ARE DIM WITH LOVE

The dachshund's trusting eyes are dim
With love for you – and tender;
The dachshund is so long and slim
And slithery and slender
That when you pat his head on Sunday
His little tail won't wag till Monday
Hoot Mon! And also Teckelheil.

- BERTHA BRIGHT RAINGER

MY OLD HOUND PACK

When my hunting here is over
    From the tall harps' golden sounds
I will steal away to hearken
    To the voices of the hounds.
When they start a phantom red fox
    On a phantom heavenly hill,
And with me, a phantom huntsman,
    Getting all the old-time thrill.
For a man who's bred to hunting
    Must forever be that way;
And he'll never know it's heaven
    Till he listens' and can say:
'there's a short low tenor,
    And a yipping ki-hi;
There's a bell-mouth ringing

That a fox has got to dies.
There's a ding-dong chop-mouth,
Always in the noise;
There's a bass with no bottom,
And a rolling gong voice.
There's a bugle with a break,
And a bugle with a scream,
And a high wailing tenor
Like a trumpet in a dream!'
-ARCHIBALD RUTLEDGE.

A PRAYER FOR ANIMALS

Hear our humble prayer O God for our friends the animals who are suffering – for all that are overworked, underfed and cruelly treated.

For any that are hunted, lost or deserted, frightened or hungry.

For all that are in pain or dying.

For all that must be put to sleep – we entreat for them Thy mercy and pity.

For all those who deal with them we ask a heart of compassion, gentle hands and kindly words.

Make us ourselves true friends of animals and may we share the blessings of the merciful for the sake of Thy Son – the tender hearted Healer – Jesus Christ our Lord, Amen!

THE DOG BELIEVED IN SIGNS

Ah! You should keep dogs – fine animals – sagacious creatures – dog of my own once – pointer – surprising instinct – out shooting one day – entering enclosure – whistled – dog stopped – whistled again – Ponto – nogo; stock still – called him – Ponto, Ponto – wouldn't move – dog transfixed – staring at a board – looked up; saw an inscription – "Gamekeeper has orders to shoot all dogs found in this enclosure" – wouldn't pass it – wonderful dog – valuable dog that – very. – Mr. Fingle, in Charles Dickens's Pickwick Paper.

CUVIER ON DOGS

"The domestic dog," said Cuvier, the great natural scientist, "is the most complete, the most singular, and the most useful conquest that man has gained in the animal world.

"The whole species has become our property; each individual belongs entirely to his master, acquires his disposition, knows and defends his property, and remains attached to until death; and all this, not through constraint or necessity, but purely by the influences of gratitude and real attachment.

"The swiftness, the strength, the sharp scent of the dog, have rendered him a powerful ally to man against the lower tribes, and were, perhaps, necessary for the establishment of the dominion of mankind over the whole animal creation. The dog is the only animal which has followed man over the whole earth."

Three Brace of Workmen.

MOTTO FOR A DOG HOUSE

I love this little house because
It offers, after dark,
A pause for rest, a rest for paws,
A place to moor my bark.
-Arthur Guiterman

REST IN PEACE

Father, in Thy starry tent,
I kneel, a humble suppliant,
A dog has died today on earth –
Of little worth
Yet very dear.
Gather him in Thy arms,
If only
For awhile,
I fear
He will be lonely,
Shield him with Thy smile.
-Wilfred J. Funk

THE LOVER OF DOGS

He made and loveth all.
Both man and bird and beast!
He prayeth best who loveth best
All things both great and small!
For the dear God who loveth us,
He made and loveth all.

-S. T. COLERIDGE.

LOYALTY

"You can't buy loyalty," they say;
I bought it though this very day.
You can't buy friendship, firm and true.
I bought sincerest friendship, too,
And truth and kindliness I got
And happiness, oh, such a lot,
So many joyous hours-to-be
Were sold with this commodity.

"I bought a life of simple faith
And love that will be mine till death;
And two brown eyes that I could see
Would not be long in knowing me.
I bought protection, I've a guard
Right now and ever afterward.
Buy human friendship? Maybe not –
You see, it was a dog I bought.

-Anne Campbell

SCOTCH DOG

A Scotsman had a dog, and each morning he gave him a penny to buy a bun. The dog deposited his penny each time in his kennel till he had five. Then off he went to the baker's shop and bought six buns for a shilling.

"MY PUP"

He's a rogue and a rascal,
A pest and a pain
And he wrecks my nylon hose.
He tracks up floors,
And nips at my heels
But I love him, goodness knows"
He annoys my friends,
When they come to call
With his shrill and noisy yap
And before they're settled in a chair
He lunges for a lap.
He simply ignores my mad protest,
And I am at a loss
It's plain for all my guests to see
Exactly who's the boss.
But when he comes at the end of day
And strikes a repentant pose,
I gather him up in my arms to rest
For I love him, goodness knows!

-HELENGA DARBY

Photo by T. Reveley, Wantage.

CH. DUSKY CRACKER. BORN 1902.

CH. DUSKY SIREN. BORN 1903.

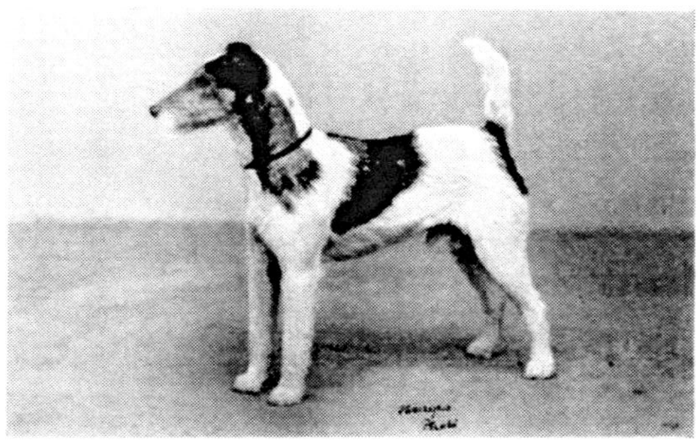

Photo by Hedges, Lytham.

CH. SOUTHBORO SALEX. BORN 1903.

Photo by Hedges, Lytham.

CH. NEWMARKET CACKLER. BORN 1905.

AN XMAS PUP

A Poodle, a Yorkie
A chubby young Pug
A smart Pekingese
With his quaint little mug,
A Manchester toy
A Papillon rare,
A beloved tarrier
That's seen everywhere –
A Maltese, Affenpinscher
Whate'er it may be,
Take your choice,
But remember –
Put a pup 'neath your tree.

-PERLA O. RICHIARDS

GOING TO THE DOGS

My grandpa notes the world's worn cogs,
And says we're going to the dogs;
His granddad in his house of logs,
Swore things were going to the dogs;
His dad, among the Flemish bogs,
Vowed things were going to the dogs;
The caveman in his queer skin togs,
Said things were going to the dogs;
But this is what I wish to state –
The dogs have had an awful wait.

-Anonymous.

MONGREL PUP FROM THE DOG SHOP

"The months crept by, as seasons will, the pup
Grew lank, unlovely as a clump of weeds;
And as he grew, our wonder grew in kind,
That one lone dog could boast so many breeds.
He had an airedales's face but that was all;
The bagging ears were those of any hound;
His silken coat was eloquent of collie;
And from his tail we knew where he'd been
found."

-MAURICE J. RONAYNE

A PROBLEM

What dog to buy?
Which breed to try?
I ponder and ponder –
I worry and sigh!
Long hair? Short hair?
Eyes deep brown, or yellow?
A hunter or collier –
Or just a good fellow?
Do I want a companion,
A guardian – a ratter?
A lap dog to cuddle?
Oh, what does it matter!
Big breed, small breed –
Black, white or brown.
I want a dog
For my very own! -NAN SWIGERT

CHRISTMAS PUPPIES

Every single puppy here
Is saying: "Choose me!"
Wagging tail, wiggling ears, -
"Don't refuse me!
"I'm your dog, wide awake!
Won't we have fun?"
Well, we have got to take
Every single one!
-NANCY BYRD TURNER

IN RETROSPECT

Our house is empty, silent now –
I never knew just how
A little dog could fill a place,
Scampering through at breakneck pace,
Scattering rugs – an upset chair –
Confusion reigned most everywhere.
But what I'd give if it could be
That he again would meet and jump on me
- Capt. Ellis Reed-Hill

Photo by T. Fall, London.

CH. DUSKY RENO. BORN 1899.

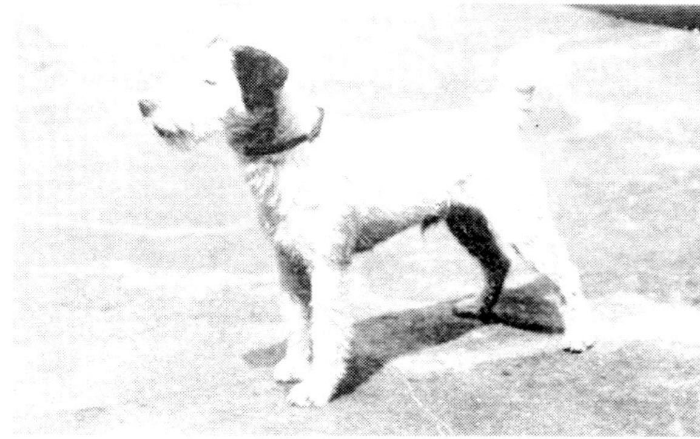

Photo by A. H. Salmon, London.

CH. COMMODORE OF NOTTS. BORN 1900.

Photo by Hussey & Son, Leeds.

CH. DUSKY ADMIRAL. BORN 1901.

Photo by A. H. Salmon, London.

CH. DUSKY GLEANER. BORN 1901.

Napoleon in Exile Recalls an Incident of the Retreat from Moscow

Suddenly I saw a dog coming out from under the clothes of a corpse. He rushed forward toward us and then returned t his retreat, uttering mournful cries. He licked the face of his master and darted toward us again; it seemed as if he was seeking aid and vengeance at the same time.

Whether it was my state of m ind, or the place, the times, the weather, the act itself, or I know not what, never has anything, on all my fields of battle, made such an impression upon me. I stopped involuntarily to contemplate the spectacle; that man, I said to myself, perhaps has friends, perhaps he has them in the camp, in his company, and yet he lies here abandoned by all except his dog.

What is man! and what the mystery of his impressions! I had ordered battles without emotion, battles which were to decide the fate of the army; I had seen, dry-eyed, movements executed which brought about the loss of a great number of our soldiers; here I was moved to tears. What is certain is that at the moment I must have been more favourably disposed toward a suppliant enemy. I better understood Achilles surrendering Hector's body to Priam's tears.

SCOTLAND'S BURNS ON DOGS

Man is the god of the dog; he knows no other; he can understand no other. And see how he worships him! With what reverence he crouches at his feet, with what love he fawns upon him! With what dependence he looks up to him! With what cheerful alacrity he obeys him!

His whole soul is wrapt up in his god! All the powers and faculties of his nature are devoted to his service! And these powers and faculties are ennobled by the intercourse.

Divines tell us that it just ought to be so with Christians – but the dog puts the Christian to shame

– ROBERT BURNS.

SCOTTISH NOVELIST ON DOGS

The Almighty who gave the dog to be the companion of our pleasures and our trials, hath invested him with a nature noble and incapable of deceit. He forgets neither friend nor foe, remembers with accuracy both benefit and in fury, and hath a share of man's intelligence but no share of man's falsehood.

– SIR WALTER SCOTT

TO BLANCO

My dear, dumb friend, low-lying there,
A willing vassal at my feet,
Glad partner of my home and fare,
My shadow in the street,

I look into your great, brown eyes,
Where love and loyal homage shine,
And wonder where the difference lies
Between your soul and mine.

For all of good that I have found
Within myself, or human kind,
Hath royally informed and crowned
Your gently heart and mind.

I scan the whole broad earth around
For that one heart which, real and true,
Bears friendship without end or hound,
And find the prize in you.

I trust you as I trust the stars;
Nor cruel loss, nor scoff, nor pride,
Nor beggary, nor dungeon bars,
Can move you from my side.

Ch. "Jack's Yarn."

A DOG AND A MAN

He was a dog
But he stayed at home
And guarded the family night and day.

He was a dog
That didn't roam.
He lay on the porch or chased the stray –
The tramps, the burglar, the hen, away;
For a dog's true heart for that household beat
At morning and evening, in cold and heat.
He was a dog.

He was a man,
And didn't stay
To cherish his wife and his children fair.

He was a man.
And every day
His heart grew callous, its love-beats rare,
He thought of himself at the close of day.
And, cigar in his fingers, hurried away
To the club, the lodge, the store, the show.
But – he had a right to go, you know.
He was a man.

- ANONYMOUS

ARGUS

When wise Ulysses, from his native coast
Long kept by wars, and long by tempests tost,
Arrived at last – poor, old, despised, alone,
To all his friends, and e'en his queen, unknown,
Changed as he was, with age, and toils, and cares,
Furrowed his rev'rend face, an d white his hairs,
In his own palace forced to ask his bread,
Scorned by those slaves his former bounty fed,
Forgot of all his own domestic crew,
His faithful dog his rightful master knew!
Unfed, unhoused, neglected, on the clay
Like an old servant, now cashiered, he lay;
And though ev'n then expiring on the plain,
Touched with resentment of ungrateful man,
And longing to behold his ancient lord again,
Him when he saw, he rose, and crawled to meet
('Twas all he could), and fawned and kissed his feet,
Seized with dumb joy; then falling by his side,
Owned his returning lord, looked up, and died.

-ALEXANDER POPE

ADVICE TO A DOG

Say truth good dogge, and doe not spare to barke,
But snarle and snappe at every sneaking thief,
Let not a Curre goe leering in the darke,
But shew thy kind, bough like a dogge, be briefe;
Lie at the door, give warning to the house,
Scratch at a flea, but care not for a louse.

Nicollo Machiavelli

(1469-1527)

PHILOSPHERS

The dogs are God's philosophers –
Though oft beset by fleas,
Because the masters, whom they love,
Eliminate not these.

Where things reversed, the human folk,
Infected with like 'bores',
Man's world were filled with dissonance,
At pain the dog ignores.

Ye-praters of real consequence,
Ye human folk 'divine'
Or so you think, forget ye not
To note a doggie's whine.

-Madge Acton Mansfield

QUOTES FROM LITERATURE

SHAKESPEARE ON DOGS

I had rather a dog and bay the moon. – Shakespeare

Cry 'havoc' and let slip the dogs of war. – Shakespeare

You play the spaniel and think with the wagging of your tongue to win me. – Shakespeare

Like Hercules himself, do what he may,
The cat will mew and dog will have his day. –
Shakespeare

> Mastiff, greyhound, mugril grim,
> Hound or spaniel, brache or lym,
> Or bobtail tike, or trundle tail.
> Shakespeare's King Lear – III-6

> My hounds are bred out of the Spartan kind . .
> and their heads are hung
> With ears that sweep away the morning dew
> Shakespeare's Midsummer Night's Dream 4-1

[illegible] [illegible] [illegible] Mischief. Tassel.

From the Painting by the late John Emms.

ITALIAN PROVERBS ON CANE (DOG)

Every dog is lion in his own house.
Cut off a dog's tail and he is still a dog.
Where there are no dogs, the fox is king.
A good dog and a good wife stay at home.

German proverb – he that represents himself as a dog must also bark like a dog.

ST. ROCHE – patron saint of dogs, on his deathbed. (13th century)

A soft caress fell on my cheek,
My hands were thrust apart.
And two big sympathizing eyes
Gazed down into my heart.

And of St. Roche's death:

Exempt from blame, he gave up his soul
As a good Christian, in the arms of his dog.

DOGGY ADVICE IN DOGGEREL

I've led a wild life;
I've earned what I've spent;
I've paid all I've borrowed;
I've lost all I've lent,
I loved a woman –
That came to an end;
Get a good dog, boys,
He'll be your real friend

ANONYMOUS

DOGGEREL

A man may smile and bid you hail,
Yet wish you to the devil;
But when a good dog wags his tail,
You know he's on the level.
- ANONYMOUS

TRIBUTE TO A SPANISH BREED

The great Pyrenees is a huge-sized dog, now fully recognised in dog shows throughout the world, yet seldom receives the praises due him. Here is an excerpt from the Shepherd Dog of the Pyrenees, written by ELLEN MURRAY.

When day at last
Broke, and the grey fog lifted, there I saw
On that ledge, against the dawning light,
My little one asleep, sitting so near
That edge that as I looked his red barette
Fell from his nodding head down the abyss.
And there, behind him, crouched Pierrot; his teeth,
His good, strong teeth, clenching the jacket brown,
Holding the child in safety. With wild bounds
Swift as the grey wolf's own I climbed the steep,
And as I reached them Pierrot beat his tail,
And looked at me, so utterly distressed.
With eyes that said: "Forgive, I could not speak,'
But never loosed his hold till my dear rogue
Was safe within my arms.

DOG BECOMES 'FIRST FRIEND'

And the woman said: 'His name is not Wild Dog any more, but the First Friend, because he will be our friend for always and always and always.'

-From one of Rudyard Kipling's stories.

MY COMFORTER

The world had all gone wrong that day
And tired and in despair,
Discouraged with the ways of life,
I sank into my chair.

A soft caress fell on my cheek,
My hands were thrust apart.
And two big sympathizing eyes
Gazed down into my heart.

I had a friend; what cared I now
For fifty worlds? I knew
One heart was anxious when I grieved –
My dog's heart, loyal, true.

"God bless him, " breathed I soft and low,
And hugged him close and tight.
One lingering lick upon my ear
And we were happy – quite.

- ANONYMOUS

MR. F. REDMOND'S CH. DUSKY CRACKER

BY CH. CACKLER OF NOTTS—DUSKY RUTH.

Photograph by Reveley, Wantage.

THE DEAD BOY'S PORTRAIT AND HIS DOG

Day after day I have come and sat
Beseechingly upon the mat,
Wistfully wondering where you are at.

Why have they placed you on the wall,
So deathly still, so strangely tall?
You do not turn from me, nor call.

Why do I never hear my name?
Why are you fastened in a frame?
You are the same, and not the same.

Away from me why do you stare
So far out in the distance where
I am not? I am here! Not there!

What has your little doggie done?
You used to whistle me to run
Beside you, or ahead, for fun!

You used to pat me, and a glow
Of pleasure through my life would go!
How is it that I shiver so?

My tail was once a waving flag
Of welcome. Now I cannot wag
It for the weight I have to drag.

I know not what has come to me.
'Tis only in my sleep I see
Things smiling as they used to be.

I do not dare to bark; I plead
But dumbly, and you never heed;
Nor my protection seem to need.

I watch the door, I watch the gate;
I am watching early, watching late,
Your doggie still! – I watch and wait.
- GERALD MASSEY

Extract from '*The Tale of Your Dog – His Origin and Need*'

Dogs are essentially gentle beings, and our imagination as well as our eyes, if only we will use them, should convince us that because of their capacity for sharing our moods and occupations, and thorough their ability to give expression to the inner workings of their minds, they are above all other animals destined to be our friends. Indeed, it is we who are in many respects the richer by this friendship. For in his dignity and command of temper; in his wisdom and patience; in his loyalty; and above all in his selflessness, a dog is a very prince of gentlemen.

– MITFORD BRICE

Material in this book has been sourced from the following titles:

Rawdon B. Lee. *A History And Description Of The Modern Dogs.* 1894
H. W. Huntington. *The Show Dog.* 1901
James Watson. *The Dog Book - A Popular History Of The Dog.* 1906
Robert Leighton. *The New Book Of The Dog.* 1907
J. Sidney Turner. *The Kennel Encyclopaedia.* 1907
J. Maxtee. *British terriers.* 1909
Darley Matheson. *Terriers.* 1922
Pierce O'conor. *Terriers For Sport.* 1924
Edward C. Ash. *The Practical Dog Book.* 1930
A. Croxton Smith. *About Our Dogs - The Breeds And Their Management.* 1931
Walter Hutchinson. *Hutchinson's Dog Encyclopaedia.* 1935
Stanley West. *The Book Of Dogs.* 1935
Various. *The Wire Haired Fox Terrier - A Complete Anthology Of The Dog.* 2010

Lightning Source UK Ltd.
Milton Keynes UK
UKOW04f1223160315

247946UK00001B/81/P

9 781447 430032